75 Sugar Flowers

Helen Penman

Search Press

A QUARTO BOOK

Published in 2014 by
Search Press Ltd
Wellwood
North Farm Road
Tunbridge Wells
Kent TN2 3DR

ISBN: 978-1-78221-057-3

QUAR:HFFC

Conceived, designed and produced by
Quarto Publishing plc
The Old Brewery
6 Blundell Street
London N7 9BH

Senior Editor: Ruth Patrick
Art Editor and Designer: Emma Clayton

Photographer: Phil Wilkins
Proofreader: Sarah Hoggett
Indexer: Helen Snaith
Picture Researcher: Sarah Bell
Art Director: Caroline Guest

Creative Director: Moira Clinch
Publisher: Paul Carslake

Colour separation by Cypress Colours (HK) Ltd
Printed by 1010 Printing International
Ltd, China

9 8 7 6 5 4 3 2 1

Contents

Foreword

I have always loved flower making, so it was a real privilege to be offered the opportunity to write a book on the subject. Trying to decide which flowers to include was not easy though, and hopefully there is a flower for everyone. I wanted to show the traditional flowers along with the more unusual ones. I also wanted to include groups of flowers that would go well together on a cake – for example, the summer flowers cake (see pages 34–35) looks impressive but is easily manageable with a little experience.

I started making cakes almost 20 years ago. I had commissioned a cake for my father's birthday, and when it came it was such poor quality that I decided I could do better myself. I got books from the library and tried things out. I enrolled at City of Bath College and took a City & Guilds course with Stephen Benison, and I now run my own cake-decorating business, Too Nice To Slice. I do hope you enjoy making the flowers in this book, and I hope to write more for you in the future!

Helen Penman

About This Book

This book starts with tools and materials, recipes and techniques, and is followed by a comprehensive directory of flowers, organized by the material from which they are made.

Techniques (pages 14–31)

Core techniques to learn before you embark on making the flowers. Here you will find recipes for all the pastes, should you wish to make your own, and techniques for piping and using buttercream, sugar paste and marzipan. There is also a brief introduction to the skills you will need to make flowers.

Core information is given in the introduction to each technique.

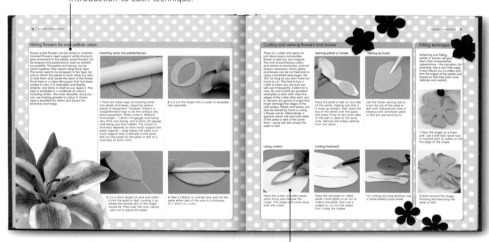

Photo steps show the technique.

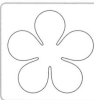 ## Templates (pages 136–139)

Many of the leaf and petal cutters used for the flowers are represented here as templates for you to trace or scan and cut out.

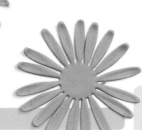

Flower directory (pages 32–135)

There are 75 flowers for you to select from in a range of materials – chocolate, marzipan, flower paste, buttercream and royal icing. One or two classic flowers – roses and lilies, for example – are demonstrated in more than one material.

Parts of this flower are inedible. Flag indicates the flowers that have inedible components, such as wire or cotton stamens.

Flagged by skill level on a scale from easy to advanced.

Written text explains the making process.

Here and there, large-scale celebration cakes are used to display the flowers.

Tools and materials listing. Basic tool kits are explained on page 14. The list includes tools and materials, including quantities of paste and how many flowers the quantity of material makes: this is always given as an approximation.

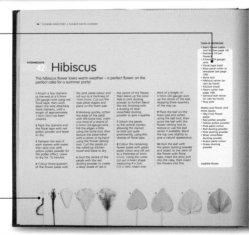

The development of the flower is shown in stages.

Flower Selector

On these pages you will find all the flowers featured in the book. Browse the selector to find the flower or flowers that would work best on the cake or cupcake you have in mind, then turn to the instructions on the referenced page.

page 41

page 42

page 43

page 44

page 46

page 47

page 48

page 50

page 51

page 52

page 53

page 54

page 55

page 56

page 58

page 59

page 60

page 62

page 63

page 66

page 65

page 68

000

page 72

page 69

page 70

page 71

page 74

page 75

page 77

page 78

page 80

page 81

page 82

page 84

page 85

page 86

page 88

page 89

page 90

page 92

page 93

page 94

page 96

page 97

page 100

page 102

page 103

page 98

page 104

page 106

page 108

page 111

page 112

page 113

page 114

page 115

page 116

page 117

page 118

page 119

page 120

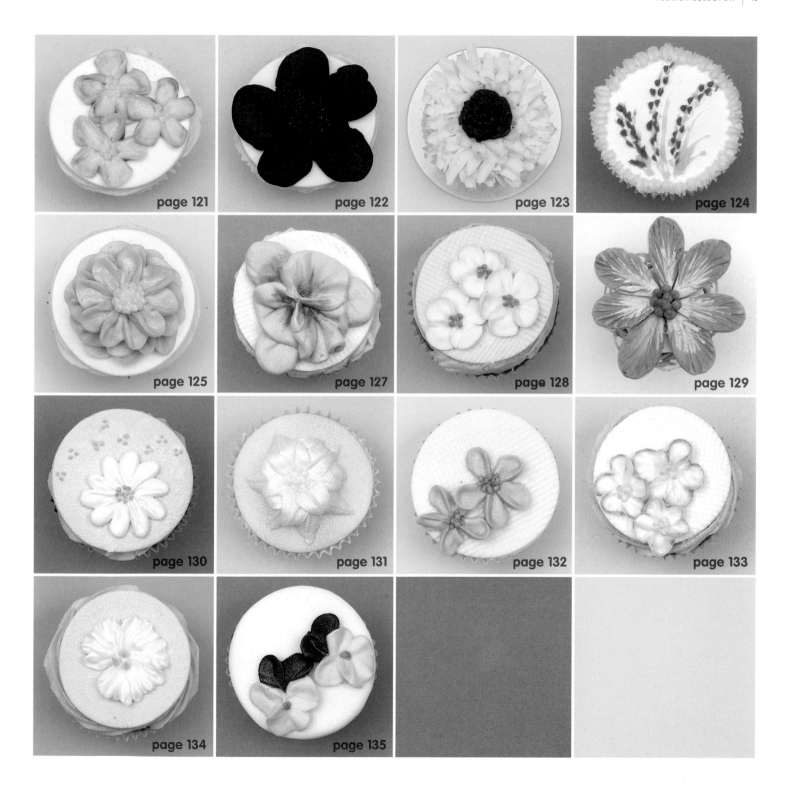

page 121

page 122

page 123

page 124

page 125

page 127

page 128

page 129

page 130

page 131

page 132

page 133

page 134

page 135

Tools and Materials

Basic Tool Kit: Chocolate

- Work board
- Foam pad
- Plastic sheets x 2
- Rolling pin
- Scalpel
- Bone tool
- Ball tool
- Flower veining tool
- Cocktail stick
- Paintbrush
- Water brush

Basic Tool Kit: Marzipan

- Work board
- Foam pad
- Plastic sheets x 2
- Rolling pin
- Scalpel
- Bone tool
- Flower veining tool
- Cocktail stick
- Paintbrush
- Water brush

Basic Tool Kit: Flower paste

- Work board
- Foam pad
- Plastic sheets x 2
- Rolling pin
- Scalpel
- Flower veining tool
- Paintbrush
- Water brush
- Former

Basic tool kits

Work board
An acrylic work board is the perfect surface to roll out paste or chocolate; it is easily washable and offers a blemish-free surface.

Foam pad
The foam pad is specially made for flower making. It is firm but soft, and has a non-stick surface. Some foam pad models have holes to support particular shapes, like Mexican hats.

Plastic sheet
To get the best from modelling chocolate or marzipan, roll out between two plastic sheets; this reduces the need to handle the paste too much, which will soften and start to melt in the case of chocolate. The sheets should be washed and dried after use.

Rolling pin
Rolling pins are available in many sizes and made of various materials. They can be textured to give different effects on the rolled-out paste, but for basic flower making a short length made from acrylic works best. A longer acrylic pin is required to roll out sugar paste for covering cakes.

Scalpel
The scalpel is a sharp, smooth, stainless-steel blade – great for cutting pastes.

Bone tool
Used to smooth curves in sugar paste when modelling and to frill petals in flower making, it is also used to soften and thin the edges of leaves and flowers.

Ball tool
This tool has many of the same features as the bone tool, having a large and small ball at each end of the handle. The ball tool will soften and cup petals without tearing the delicate paste.

Flower veining tool
The flower veining tool, or Dresden tool, is used to smooth and flute paste, using the back of the tool. It is also ideal for creating finely detailed veins on leaves and flowers.

Cocktail stick
The cocktail stick has three uses – to support a flower while it is drying, as a texturing/frilling tool, and to add colour from a paste pot to the medium.

Paintbrush
Paintbrushes should include a broad one for dusting flowers and one that has fine bristles to allow for detailed and accurate painting.

Water brush
A water brush is a paintbrush with its own water reservoir contained within the brush. Clean the brush and change the water regularly.

Former
A former is any support for a flower, petal or leaf while it is drying. The device may be shop-bought, with cups for drying curved shapes or spaces for hanging flowers, or it may be improvised with kitchen towel rolled into elongated sausage shapes.

General tools

Palette knife
A palette knife is a flat-bladed knife, with either a straight or an angled handle. This knife comes in several sizes, from very small to assist in lifting delicate items onto a cake to extra large to smooth soft paste such as buttercream over cakes and cupcakes.

Piping bag
The piping bag is specifically designed to hold a soft medium such as buttercream, royal icing or jam. It is usually used in conjunction with a piping tube.

Piping tube
This is a stainless-steel cone-shaped tube with ends of different designs that texture the soft medium as it is being piped. Use with a piping bag. When the medium is extruded through the tube it takes on the shape of the tube, holding that shape to create attractive finishes to cakes and cupcakes.

Every sugarcrafter has their favourite tools for making flowers. Several tools will do more than one job and there are some that are indispensable. When buying tools, buy the best you can afford. There are also general kitchen tools that are useful when making flowers.

Cutters come in many shapes.

Cutters

Flower and leaf cutters are made of stainless steel, so they keep their shape well, are easy to clean and the edge does not blunt quickly. The cutter will be shaped to emulate the flower/leaf/petal that is being made, and there are hundreds to choose from in various sizes, depending on the size of flower being made.

Pizza wheel

This tool is perfect to use for long sections of paste requiring trimming, because it cuts without tearing the paste.

Moulds

Moulds save time, since they will shape a piece of paste quickly without the need to model or sculpt. These are excellent if you are short of time or a beginner, but they can be expensive.

Veiners

Veiners are usually made from soft material that is food safe and non-stick. They generally come in two sides so the petal/leaf is veined on both sides at the same time. Veiners vary in price depending on the quality of the veining, some made to be a true representation of that particular petal/leaf, while others are more impressionistic.

Templates

Templates are a quick solution to the lack of a specific cutter. Make them from stiff card and cut around using a pizza wheel or scalpel.

Celstick

A non-stick nylon stick, similar to a cocktail stick and approved for use with food. The Celstick works in a similar way to a cocktail stick for thinning and frilling without the risk of it sticking to the paste and tearing the petal or leaf.

Materials

Food-grade wire

Cake decorating and sugarcraft flower wires are available in standard lengths of 30.5cm (12in) and various thicknesses (gauges) and colours. They are inedible.

Stamens

Stamens are made from cotton specifically for making sugar flowers more lifelike. They come in an array of colours, shapes and sizes to suit whatever flower is being made. Cotton stamens are inedible. Edible stamens can be made as an alternative.

Posy picks

A posy pick is a small, hollow cone made of food-grade plastic. The pick is inserted into a cake or cupcake so that wired flowers can be used to decorate the cake without the wires or floral tape coming into contact with the cake. The non-edible wired flowers and the pick can be easily removed before the cake is eaten.

Floral tape

This is a paper-and-latex tape used to bind flower wires. It is available in various shades of green, red, brown and white. To create a narrower tape, cut the strip into three (see page 31). Dust white tape with dusting powder colour to complement the flower. Floral tape is inedible and should not come into contact with the cake or cupcake.

Pollen powder

Pollen powder is a granular food colour ideal for colouring stamen heads and creating a textured effect on icing. Simply shake pollen powder over the moistened article or surface. Pollen powder gives a lifelike pollen effect to stamens. If this is not available, an effective solution is to use semolina with dusting powder added.

Food colours

Powder food colour is used when you don't want to alter the consistency of the medium. This is important when using modelling chocolate or marzipan where a liquid-based colour would make the paste more sticky and unworkable. Use liquid, gel or paste food colour when the medium will not alter significantly by the introduction of extra liquid. These food colours will give a deeper colour than can be achieved with powder.

Dusting powder

Dusting powder is available in an enormous range of shades. The powder can be used to colour paste – either because you want a light shade or because the medium warrants the use of powder – or it can be dusted on a finished piece. Some dusting powders have special effects added, such as glitter, that enhance the appearance.

Cocoa butter

Cocoa butter is a hard, pale yellow edible vegetable fat extracted from the cocoa bean. It is used to make chocolate, but also as a base for painting on cakes, cupcakes and chocolate flowers. It has a low melting point so melts easily over heated water. Melted cocoa butter blends well with dusting powders to create paint.

From left: paintbrushes, flower veining tool, ball tool and bone tool.

Basic Recipes

The pastes used in this book are easily found in local food shops or specialist cake-decorating outlets. However, if you want to make them yourself, you will find all the recipes you need on the following pages.

Sugar paste

Sugar paste is a cake covering that rolls out smoothly. It is a sweet paste that sets firmly on the outside, but is still soft enough to cut with a knife. It can easily be coloured using a paste or liquid colour.

Ingredients

Makes 1kg (2lb 4oz)

- 4 tbsp cold water
- 4 tsp/1 sachet powdered gelatin (you can use the vegetarian version if you prefer)
- 125ml (4 fl oz) liquid glucose
- 1 tbsp glycerol
- 1kg (2lb 4oz) icing sugar

1 Place the cold water in a bowl, sprinkle the gelatin over and soak until spongy.

2 Stand the bowl over a pan of hot but not boiling water and stir until the gelatin has dissolved.

3 Add the glucose and glycerol, stirring until well blended and runny.

4 Sift the icing sugar into a large bowl. Make a well in the centre and slowly pour in the liquid ingredients, stirring constantly.

5 Mix well, then turn out onto a surface dusted with icing sugar. Knead until smooth, sprinkling with extra icing sugar if the paste becomes excessively sticky.

6 The sugar paste can be used straight away or wrapped and stored in a plastic bag until needed.

Sugar paste cake covering with flower paste flowers.

Marzipan

Marzipan is a grainy paste. This is a delicious and straightforward marzipan recipe that can be given different flavours with the addition of cinnamon or orange zest. Try a touch of brandy for a special flavouring during the holiday season.

Ingredients

Makes 500g (1lb 2oz)

- 250g (9oz) icing sugar
- 250g (9oz) finely ground blanched almonds
- 2 egg whites
- ½ tsp salt
- ½ tsp almond extract

1 Sift all the dry ingredients together, add the egg whites and almond extract and mix with a wooden spoon.

2 Store in a sealed bag overnight in the fridge.

Flower paste

Flower paste is a firm paste used for making flowers that need support. It has gum tragacanth added. If you don't want to make the whole paste from scratch you can add 1 tsp to 250g (½lb) sugar paste, which will give you a workable paste in three hours.

Ingredients

Makes 500g (1lb 2oz)
- 500g (1lb 2oz) icing sugar
- 1 tbsp gum tragacanth
- 1½ tbsp cold water
- 2 tsp powdered gelatin
- 2 tsp liquid glucose
- 1 tbsp white vegetable fat
- 1 medium egg white

1 Sift the icing sugar and gum tragacanth into the mixing bowl of a heavy-duty food mixer, if available.

2 Put the water in a bowl, sprinkle the gelatin over and soak until spongy. Stand the bowl over a pan of hot water and stir until the gelatin has dissolved.

4 Add the glucose and white vegetable fat to the gelatin, stirring until all the ingredients are melted and mixed.

5 Add the mixture to the icing sugar, along with the egg white. Beat the mixture very slowly – it will look a dark cream colour at this stage, due to the gelatin.

7 Increase the speed to maximum until the paste becomes white and stretchy.

8 Grease your hands and remove the paste from the bowl. Pull and stretch the paste, then knead together. Place in a plastic bag and store in an airtight container. Leave the paste to mature for at least 24 hours.

Modelling chocolate

Modelling chocolate can be made using milk or dark chocolate; however, to be able to colour modelling chocolate, you will need to work with a base of white modelling chocolate. Always use powder colour with modelling chocolate, since liquid colour will make the paste too sticky and unworkable.

Ingredients

Makes 500g (1lb 2oz)
- 350g (12oz) white chocolate chips
- 4 fl oz (125ml) corn syrup or liquid glucose

1 Melt the chocolate slowly in the microwave, giving it blasts of 10–20 seconds at a time until it is all melted. Alternatively, melt in a bowl held over a pan of hot water. Stir well to distribute the heat throughout the whole of the melted chocolate.

2 Warm up the corn syrup so that, when the two mix together, the syrup doesn't cool the chocolate.

3 Blend the two together, then pour onto cling film. Cover with the cling film and leave to cool for two to three hours.

4 Once cool, knead until smooth, then place in a sealed bag until required.

Buttercream

Buttercream is a delicious, fluffy icing that is used as a filling or topping for cupcakes and cakes. Buttercream is versatile and can be piped into delicious flower decorations that are tasty and wonderful to look at. Buttercream becomes crispy on the outside but still soft and creamy inside.

The consistency needs to be firmer for flower piping, so less milk will be required, but a thinner buttercream is ideal for a crumb coat on a cake. The flavour of the buttercream can be altered by adding different extracts, such as peppermint, lemon, coconut or coffee, and the colour can be changed using paste food colours. If you want a light-coloured icing, use only clear flavourings, but remember that darker colours will deepen on setting. The addition of cocoa powder to the finished buttercream will make a delicious chocolate buttercream.

Buttercream is affected by heat and humidity – buttercreamed cakes can be left for three to four days at room temperature, but high temperature will cause buttercream to soften and melt. Don't be tempted to refrigerate, since this will cause condensation on the icing and colours will bleed.

Ingredients
Makes 850g (1lb 14oz)
- 125g (4½oz) softened butter
- 125g (4½oz) white vegetable vegetable fat
- 600g (1lb 5oz) icing sugar
- 1 tsp vanilla extract
- Milk (optional depending on consistency)

Plain buttercream

Combine the ingredients in a large bowl and beat on a low speed until well blended, or hand mix with a wooden spoon. Continue for five minutes until creamy. Keep the icing covered to prevent the icing from drying and becoming crispy. The buttercream can be kept in the refrigerator for up to six weeks – rebeat it before using.

Two-tone buttercream – method 1

1 Prepare the buttercream.

2 Using paste food colour, paint a streak up one side of the piping bag, then fill the bag with buttercream using a palette knife.

3 Start piping and the paste colour will colour the buttercream as it is squeezed out.

Two-tone buttercream – method 2

1 Prepare the buttercream.

2 Split into two batches and colour each to suit the theme of your cake or cupcake.

3 Fill one side of the piping bag with one colour and fill the other side with the other colour.

4 Start piping and the two colours will come through the tube.

Royal icing

Royal icing can be used to cover a cake, secure decorations onto a cake, or pipe designs or sugar flowers. When using royal icing as a cake covering, the addition of glycerol to the recipe is important, since this will stop the icing from drying too hard and making it impossible to slice.

There are many different recipes for royal icing, but the most common is made with egg whites. If you are in a hurry, royal icing powder is now also widely available – it is quick to make up with the addition of water – or a ready-made royal icing can also be bought.

Ingredients

Makes 450g (1lb)

- 450g (1lb) icing sugar
- 3 large egg whites or egg white substitute
- ⅛ tsp cream of tartar

1 Firstly, ensure that all utensils are free from grease, including any yolk in the egg white because this will stop the royal icing forming.

2 Sift the icing sugar into a clean metallic bowl using a fine sieve (this avoids large granules of icing sugar getting into the mix and clogging the piping tube) and pour in the egg whites.

3 Whisk gently, then add the cream of tartar, slowly increasing the speed of the mixer or beating with a metal spoon or palette knife.

4 Beat on high speed until the icing is glossy and forms stiff peaks when the whisk is lifted from the icing, or beat with a metal spoon or palette knife.

5 Royal icing will dry quickly and form a crust, which makes it impossible to pipe without clogging up the piping tube. So, cover the surface of the royal icing with a lightly dampened piece of kitchen towel. This will stop the crust from forming and ensure that there is no wastage. The icing can be stored in the fridge in an airtight container for up to 24 hours, but if using egg white substitute, it can be kept for up to two weeks in the refrigerator. Always rebeat before use. Flowers that are made using royal icing can be stored in an airtight container for several months.

Piping techniques

The techniques in this book for piping with royal icing or buttercream are the same, so if you prefer to pipe a flower in royal icing but the instructions are for buttercream, you can easily use royal icing and the results will be as good! If you have previously been piping with buttercream, you will need to meticulously wash your equipment to remove the grease before using royal icing.

When using royal icing to pipe flowers, some will require a softer consistency of icing than others, giving a different texture when piped. A stiffer icing will suit flowers with rough edges such as the carnation (see page 113) or the rose (see page 112), but again the rose can be made with a softer icing to create a different flower.

Basic Techniques

Making a piping bag

Ready-made piping bags in either plastic, polyester or silicone can be bought and are great time savers, although they can be costly. The cloth bags can be washed several times and reused, and are ideal for large quantities. Piping bags can be made from flat, square sheets of greaseproof paper and of any size suitable to the need for the bag, although for large quantities of buttercream a plastic or cloth bag will be easier to use.

1 Always make greaseproof bags using a double layer of paper, because the paper gets rather soft. Take a square of paper and fold it in half to create a triangle.

2 Take the two points at either end of the long side and twist them over each other to form a cone, with the third point at the top of the cone.

3 Fold the top over to secure the paper in place.

4 Snip off the end of the point and insert the piping tube.

Filling and covering a cake with buttercream

A cake can be filled and completely covered with buttercream as the decorative finish; alternatively, buttercream can be used as a sticking agent if the cake is to be finished in sugar paste. If the cake is going to be completely finished with buttercream it is better to cover it first with a thin layer of buttercream as a crumb coat, place in the refrigerator for 20 minutes, then cover the cake with the final layer of buttercream without the worry that crumbs will get into it and spoil the finished covering. If you prefer you can pipe the buttercream, creating a patterned finish to the cake, rather than applying with a palette knife.

1 Slice the cake in half and fill the cake with buttercream – add a jam filling also, if you wish. Place the top layer of cake on top and press together.

2 Apply a thin layer of buttercream over the whole of the cake as a crumb coat, then place in the refrigerator for 20 minutes.

3 Cover the whole cake with softened buttercream, using a palette knife to spread a thick, smooth layer over the whole of the side of the cake.

4 Use a buttercream comb to create textures on the side of the cake or, if you prefer, stick shredded coconut, chocolate chips, curls, nuts, etc. to the side of the cake.

Filling cupcakes

Cupcakes are delicious morsels of sponge cake wrapped in a paper case. Traditionally, cupcakes were covered with buttercream, or the centre cut out and filled with buttercream and the centre popped back on top. Cupcakes can be filled with jam using a piping tube, then topped with buttercream (see right).

1 Place the piping tube in the bottom of the piping bag. If you are using a tube with a relatively small hole, you may want to sift the jam first to remove any lumps that might get stuck. If the tube has a large end, sifting is not necessary.

2 Fill the bag with jam, then push it into the top of the cupcake and squeeze a small amount of jam into the cupcake.

Covering cupcakes with buttercream

Buttercream can be piped onto cupcakes to give a decorative finish – a quick and simple way to create a delightful topping. Alternatively, the piping can be used as a base for further decoration. Or the buttercream can be applied to the top of the cupcake using a palette knife. The cupcakes can then be decorated with flowers. If piping, place a star piping tube into the piping bag. The bag needs to be of a large size to accommodate a sufficient amount of buttercream – there is nothing more annoying than trying to refill the bag. Fill the bag three-quarters full of buttercream, fold over the top, and you are ready to pipe.

Piping up to a point

Start by piping around the edge of the cupcake, working inward and upward with successive layers, and finishing with a point.

Piping flat

Start by piping in the centre of the cupcake, working around in a spiral fashion to the edge of the cake.

Applying with a palette knife

Take a dessertspoon of buttercream and, using a flat palette knife, spread liberally over the top of the cake.

Ruffled effect

Work from left to right on the cupcake and pipe in lines, working backward and forward to give a ruffled appearance.

Mini swirls

Pipe 'dots' of buttercream over the top of the cupcake with a star piping tube, completely covering it for a swirly appearance.

Covering cupcakes with sugar paste

Covering cupcakes in rolled sugar paste leaves a smooth, crisp finish, which can be embossed or crimped to add feature – but take care to roll quite thinly because the sweetness of the sugar paste layer may overshadow the flavour of the cake. Use a thin layer of buttercream under the sugar paste layer to adhere the paste to the cake.

1 Prepare the cupcake with a thin layer of buttercream, either piped neatly or spread over with a palette knife.

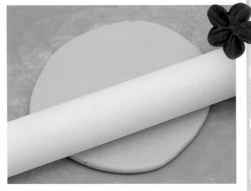

2 Roll out the sugar paste to your preferred thickness, 3–5mm (⅛–³⁄₁₆in).

3 Cut out a circle of the sugar paste, using a round cutter large enough to cover the top of the cupcake.

4 Place the disk of paste on top of the cupcake and press lightly. Smooth the paste with a cake smoother or a pad of the paste to polish and smooth the cupcake top neatly.

Covering a cake with rolled sugar paste or marzipan

Rolled sugar paste is sweet icing that can be kneaded from quite a hard block into a soft pliable sheet of paste to drape over the cake or cupcake and create a smooth, clean finish that is not possible to create with any other icing.

The covering is placed over a cake after it has been covered thinly in a buttercream layer. This smooths out any indentations, but also helps to stick the sugar paste to the cake.

Sugar paste can be embossed, textured, crimped and indented while it is still soft, but over a period of hours the paste will become firm on the outside but still soft under the surface. It is important to remember to wrap any unused paste in a plastic bag to stop it from drying out and crumbling away.

Marzipan is a paste that is made from almonds, sugar and egg and is a delicious covering usually used on a fruit cake. It seals in the moisture and provides a smooth surface to then decorate the cake. Marzipan can be treated in the same way as sugar paste to cover a cake, but it is rolled out slightly thicker – around 1cm (½in) thick.

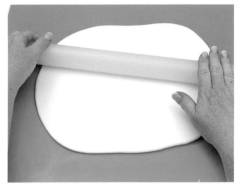

1 Knead the paste until soft and pliable. Place on a work surface lightly dusted with icing sugar and roll out with a rolling pin. Lift the paste up frequently on the rolling pin to ensure that it isn't sticking. Don't turn the paste over – keep the rolled surface uppermost – this will be the outer surface of your cake.

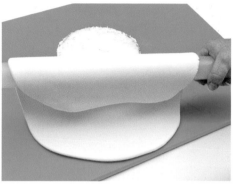

2 Continue rolling out the paste until you have a uniform thickness of around 3–6mm (⅛–¼in). Lift the paste on the rolling pin and drape it over the cake. Use your hands to smooth the paste around the cake sides.

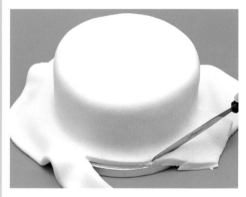

3 Use a knife to cut off the excess paste, roughly first, then go around the cake again, trimming neatly to the base of the cake.

4 Use a cake smoother to create a neat, smooth finish to the sides and top of the cake.

5 Finish the cake covering by smoothing over with a pad of the paste – running it all over the cake will polish the paste and give a natural shine.

Flower Techniques

Making flowers in flower paste

Flower paste flowers can be rolled very thinly, creating very realistic flowers for cupcakes and cakes. They can be wired or unwired and arranged in sprays or singly to make an ordinary cake into a talking point. There are dozens of cutters available to make every conceivable flower; however, this is a considerable expense. In this book some cutters have been used, but also templates that can be found at the back of the book (see pages 136–139). Try to buy or find a real flower to refer to when making a sugar flower – you will find it easier to make more realistic. If this isn't possible, look the flower up on the Internet. Follow the instructions for each individual flower in Chapter 2, but basic techniques are explained in detail on the following pages.

Mexican hat method for pulled flowers and cutter flowers

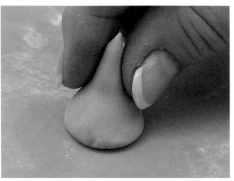

This technique is used for flowers such as stephanotis (see page 88) or jasmine (see page 55).

1 Take a small pinch of paste and roll it into a ball.

2 Start twisting the paste on the top while flattening the base.

Using modelling chocolate and marzipan

Modelling chocolate and marzipan need a little extra care when making flowers. The pastes are quite sticky and can become difficult to shape and mould if they become too warm from being worked. Unwired flowers are generally made from marzipan or chocolate – wiring with this sort of medium would be difficult because the paste has to be rolled more thickly than flower paste and the wire would not be able to support it easily. When colouring the pastes work quickly then wrap in a plastic bag to allow the paste to cool and firm up again. The process of colouring will have made the paste warm and soft and started melting the oils within the paste.

1 Take a piece of white modelling chocolate and place between two sheets of plastic. A plastic sleeve, similar to one that notes can be filed in, is perfect; slit it down two sides, leaving one side attached. This makes it easier to get to the chocolate if necessary.

2 Roll out the paste between the two sheets of plastic – this will ensure that it will not stick to the work surface and the use of icing sugar is not required.

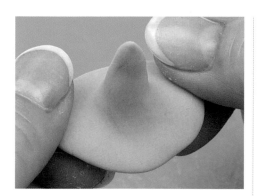

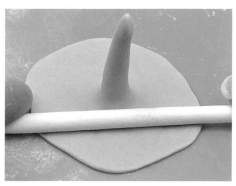

3 Continue pulling the paste, thinning out the base.

4 Use a cocktail stick or Celstick to flatten the base further.

5 At this point you can use a cutter to shape the base into the flower shape, use a template (see pages 136–139) or cut the shape freehand using a scalpel.

Wiring flowers for non-edible cakes

Flower paste flowers can be wired or unwired. Unwired flowers need support while drying to give movement to the petals; wired flowers can be shaped and positioned to look as realistic as possible. The petals and leaves can be wired together, then taped using floral tape. The wires need to be wrapped in the tape not only to attach the petals to each other but also to hide them and create the stem of the flower. Floral tape is a crêpe-like paper that has been coated in wax; it is reversible and slightly stretchy, and sticks to itself as you apply it. The tape is available in a multitude of colours, including white – the most versatile, since you can use dusting powder to colour it. Green tape is excellent for stems and brown for branches and twigs.

Inserting wires into petals/leaves

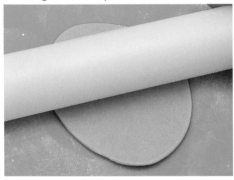

1 There are many ways of inserting wires into petals and leaves, requiring various pieces of equipment. However, there is a straightforward way to do this without any extra equipment. Wires come in different thicknesses – 1.6mm (14-gauge) wire being very thick and strong, and 0.2mm (33-gauge) wire being very fine indeed. The choice of thickness depends on how much support the paste requires – large leaves will need a lot more support than a delicate orchid petal. Roll out the paste for the petal or leaf to a thickness of 3mm (⅛in).

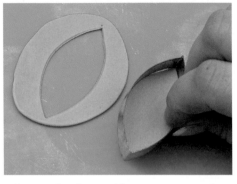

2 Cut out the shape with a cutter or template (see opposite).

3 Cut a short length of wire and insert it into the petal or leaf, running it up where the central vein of the shape would be. Press over the wire, taking care not to pierce the paste.

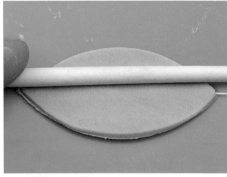

4 Take a Celstick or cocktail stick and roll the paste either side of the wire to a thickness of 1–2mm (1/32–1/16in).

Cutting and veining flowers and leaves

There is a cutter and veiner for just about every conceivable flower or leaf you can imagine. The cost of purchasing cutters and veiners is enormous, and not always necessary. Many petals and leaves can be cut freehand or using a template (see pages 136–139), as long as you don't have too many to cut. The time to buy a cutter is when you are sure you will use it frequently. Cutters for a rose, lily and orchid are excellent examples to start with. Wipe the edges of the cutter after each use to remove any grains of sugar that might damage the edges of the next shape. Petals and leaves can also be veined by hand or using a flower veiner. Alternatively, a general veiner will vein both sides of the petal or leaf at the same time – some will also shape the petal or leaf.

Veining petals or leaves

Place the petal or leaf on one side of the veiner, making sure that it is lined up straight, then place the top of the veiner over the paste and press firmly to vein both sides of the leaf or petal at the same time Remove the shape carefully from the veiner.

Veining by hand

Use the flower veining tool to score the top of the petal or leaf with characteristic lines in keeping with whichever petal or leaf you are working on.

Using cutters

Place the cutter on rolled paste, press firmly and remove the cutter. The shape will come away with the cutter.

Cutting freehand

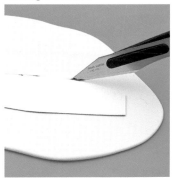

Place the template on rolled paste. Hold lightly so as not to indent the paste, then use a scalpel to cut out the shape. Don't drag the scalpel.

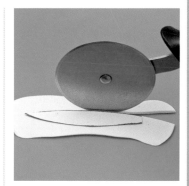

For cutting out long sections, use a metal-bladed pizza wheel.

Frilling technique

Softening and frilling petals or leaves will give them their characteristic appearance – the carnation, for example, has a very frilly edge. It also allows you to soften and thin the edges of the petals and leaves so that they look more delicate and realistic.

1 Place the shape on a foam pad. Use a ball tool, bone tool or cocktail stick to soften or frill the edge of the shape.

2 Work around the shape, thinning and texturing the petal or leaf.

Creating flower centres

Making non-edible wired stamens

The centre of the flower is generally made separately to the petals. If you are using a non-edible centre, make sure you tell the recipient of the cake. Wired flowers are never eaten, since they contain the wires within the petals. Stamen centres can be shop bought and a wide array is available; however, they can also be made using cotton thread and dusted with pollen powder – a granular food colour available in different colours – to represent pollen.

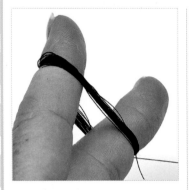

1 Take hold of a cotton reel in one hand and wrap the cotton around two fingers of the other hand.

2 Insert a hooked wired into each end of the threads, twisting and securing. Cut the threads halfway between the two wires.

3 Tape the ends of the wires with floral tape, incorporating the folded threads to secure in place.

4 Dampen the ends of the threads and dust with pollen powder. If coloured stamens are required, dust them with an appropriate dusting powder.

Making edible flower centres

There are moulds available for making various sizes of edible flower centres, with different stamen patterns to suit any flower.

Alternative methods

Alternatively, edible centres can be handmade with the use of a few simple kitchen implements.

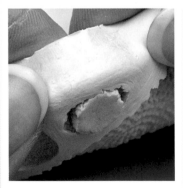

1 Roll the paste into a ball and flatten it. Place in the mould and press firmly. Turn the mould upside down and tap hard to release the paste without distorting the shape.

2 Place the centre into the flower and secure with edible glue or a dot of royal icing.

1 If you don't have a mould available, use a sieve to texture by pressing several times, turning the sieve after each one.

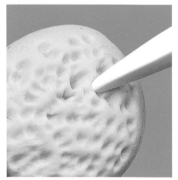

2 Using the pointed end of a flower veining tool or a cocktail stick, prick the paste several times to create a textured surface.

Creating edible stamens from noodles

Edible stamens are made from flower paste or Chinese noodles. The following steps show how to make edible stamens from store-cupboard noodles and pollen powder. Flower paste stamens can also be made by rolling out flower paste and cutting thin strips. Once these are dry, dampen the tip with water, and dip into pollen powder. Alternatively, there are stamen moulds on sale that make lifelike stamens. One method of attaching stamens is described here. Follow the cotton stamen instructions on the relevant flower but replace cotton stamens with edible noodle stamens instead.

1 Soak the noodles in hot water for one hour. If coloured stamens are required add food colour to the water before soaking. Sugar can also be added to the water but this is optional Lay the noodles out flat on greaseproof paper until dry – this will take a couple of days. When completely dry, store in an airtight container ready for use.

2 Dampen the tip of the noodle and dip it into some pollen powder.

3 The stamens can then be inserted into the centre of a flower. It is best to do this while the petals or centre of the flower are still soft.

Drying petals and leaves

Wired petals and leaves are supported with their wires in the position for drying, so actual support is not required, but a useful piece of equipment is a wired drying stand that allows you to stand the wired piece up or hang it upside down while it dries. Unwired flowers require support until dry. You can use foam or kitchen towel rolled into cylinders; alternatively, there are pieces of drying equipment that can be purchased.

Use rolled-up kitchen towel as a support system.

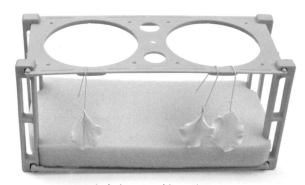

A drying stand in action.

Unwired flowers can also be placed in shaped formers, either commercially purchased for this purpose or made from aluminium foil shaped to support the flower.

Working with colour

Colouring with dusting powder

1 Load a paintbrush with dusting powder from the pot. Don't tip the powder directly from the pot, because it may all drop out and be wasted.

2 Place the powder on a piece of kitchen towel and work it onto the brush.

3 Dust the intended spot on the petal or leaf with the loaded paintbrush, taking care not to get powder onto any other area.

4 Build up the colour with further layers of powder, rather than adding too much at one time.

Making a coloured paint

1 Using a paintbrush, place a small amount of dusting powder in a palette.

2 Add a few drops of clear alcohol and mix with the paintbrush. You can use water, but it takes longer to dry and may soften the paste while it dries. Alcohol evaporates quickly, so is the liquid of choice.

3 Apply to the petal or leaf using a paintbrush. If the paint starts to thicken, add more drops of clear alcohol.

4 Build up the colour as you paint. You can apply both pale and dark colours to add detail and depth to petal or leaf.

Colour mixing with paste colour

Use paste colour to colour flower paste, buttercream, royal icing and sugar paste, but not chocolate or marzipan.

1 Dip the end of a clean cocktail stick into the paste colour and add it to your paste.

2 Knead the paste to blend the colour evenly.

Colour mixing with dusting powder

Use dusting powder with flower paste, chocolate and marzipan, not buttercream or royal icing.

1 Use a palette knife to place the powder on the flower paste.

2 Knead the paste to blend the colour evenly.

Using non-edible floral tape

Floral tape is available in a width of 1cm (½in). It is quite difficult to get a neat finish with this width, so it is a good idea to slice the tape into three thinner tapes. Unreel a section around 10cm (4in) long and use scissors to snip this into three 10cm (4in) lengths.

1 Attach one end of the tape to the tip of the wire, then pull the tape slightly with one hand while holding the wire with the other.

2 Twist the wire while maintaining the tension on the tape, allowing the tape to cover the wire. Continue along the length of the wire.

Flower
Directory

A directory of 75 flowers organized into five different mediums. Perfect flowers to stand alone or be grouped together to make elegant decorations for celebration cakes.

Summer flowers

A pastel-themed summer garden
celebration cake, featuring lilac,
apple blossom, poppies and
buttercups. The cake is finished with
a simple fringe of grass around the
base. Sprinkle loose petals across
the cake's surface.

Spring flowers

A spring-themed, two-tier cake,
decorated with chocolate flowers:
daffodils, hydrangea, primrose and
lily of the valley. Strips of balls
in different colours and sizes
link the displays together.

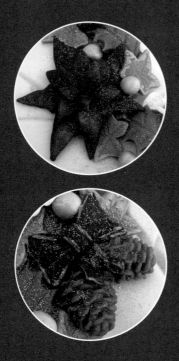

Christmas flowers

Shaped like an ivy leaf and the board
decorated with snowballs and
nonpareils, this Christmas cake
features marzipan, ivy dusted around
the edges with gold, Christmas
roses, pine cones, a poinsettia, deep
red bows, stars and gold baubles.
A perfect cake for Christmas Day.

Chocolate Flowers

Tools & Materials

- Basic chocolate tool kit, minus bone tool (see page 14)
- Ball tool
- Large 5cm (2in) rose petal cutter or template (see page 136)

Makes one flower
- 25g (⅞oz) white modelling chocolate
- Pale orange dusting powder

Rose

The elegant rose is made of chocolate, a perfect medium to show off the intricacies of the flower.

1 Colour the modelling chocolate with pale orange dusting powder, and leave it to firm up.

2 Roll out the chocolate between the plastic sheets to a thickness of 3mm (⅛in).

3 Using a cutter or template, cut out 10 rose petal shapes and place on a foam pad.

4 Use the ball tool to soften the edges, but don't press too hard – the chocolate is soft and you may make a hole.

5 Collect the remnants and shape into a cone. Insert the cocktail stick into the base.

6 Attach two petals to the cone using water and wrap around the cone neatly, overlapping one petal onto the other at one side and underlapping at the other side. Secure at the base, but allow the petals at the top to open up slightly.

7 Attach three more petals, overlapping on one side and underlapping on the other as before, and curling the petals out.

8 Attach the remaining five petals in the same way, curling the petal tops out further to give a full rose appearance.

9 Leave to dry, then remove from the cocktail stick and place on your cake or cupcake.

3   4   4   5   6   7   8

INTERMEDIATE

02 Orchid

The orchid, elegant petals interestingly arranged; chocolate is the perfect medium to show this flower at its best.

1 Colour the chocolate with the blue or purple dusting powder and leave it to firm up. Roll out the chocolate between two plastic sheets to a thickness of 2–3mm (1/16–1/8in), then cut out the petals using the cutters or templates: two large oval petals for the base of the flower, three smaller petals for the top section and the central section.

2 Use the ball tool to soften the edges of the five petals.

3 Use the cocktail stick to frill the edges of the petals slightly.

4 Soften the central section of the flower with the bone tool, rubbing the tool over the whole shape, enlarging it slightly and also gently curling the parts of the shape inward.

5 Position the three smaller upper petals on the cake or cupcake and secure in place with a dot of buttercream or royal icing. Then position the two large oval petals underneath at either side of the centre of the flower, using dots of buttercream or royal icing to secure.

6 Place the central section on the centre of the flower, again securing with dots of buttercream or royal icing.

7 Take a pinch of chocolate and roll into a small teardrop shape that will fit inside the centre of the flower. Indent down each side of the teardrop and attach the pointed end to the centre of the flower.

8 When the flower is dry (two to four hours), dust it with the blue or purple dusting powder and add silver snowflake dusting powder for shimmer.

1 2 3 3 4 7

Tools & Materials

- Basic chocolate tool kit (see page 14)
- Lily cutters or template (see page 136)
- Lily petal veiner (optional)
- Cotton stamens x 6

Makes one flower
- 30g (1oz) white modelling chocolate
- Brown dusting powder
- Orange dusting powder
- Kitchen towel

Inedible stamens
For edible stamens, see page 29

Lily **INTERMEDIATE** 03

The lily offers simple understated elegance.

1 Roll a pea-size chocolate ball into a sausage shape and insert a cocktail stick through the end to make the pistil.

2 Attach the stamens around the pistil and cocktail stick, using water and a tiny strip of modelling chocolate if necessary.

3 Dust the stamens and pistil with the brown dusting powder. Leave to allow the pistil to firm up.

4 Colour the remaining modelling chocolate with orange dusting powder and leave it to firm up.

5 Roll out the chocolate between the plastic sheets to a medium thickness of 2–3mm (¹⁄₁₆–¹⁄₈in). Using the cutter or template, cut out three broad petals and three narrow petals.

6 Place on a foam pad and soften and thin the edges with the bone tool, taking care not to press too hard and tear the petal.

7 If using the veiner, press and vein each petal. If not, use the flower veining tool and draw the pointed end of the tool down the centre of each petal, then do the same down either side of the central line.

8 Place the veined petals on the foam pad again and soften the edges, this time with the side of the cocktail stick, allowing the grain of the stick to texture the petals a little to add depth.

9 Attach the three broad petals first to the central stamen arrangement using water. Hold for a few seconds until secure, then set aside, supporting the petals in a curved-out position until firm.

10 Attach the narrower three petals in the same way, supporting them again until set.

11 When the flower is dry, pull out the cocktail stick and position the flower on your cake or cupcake

12 Dust the petals with orange dusting powder.

3   3   5   6   8

EASY

04 Peony

The peony comes in shades of bright pink, red, yellow or white. They can have few petals to the bloom or many petals, giving a full, blowsy flower.

1 Roll out half of the modelling chocolate between the plastic sheets to a thickness of 3mm (⅛in). Cut out three petal shapes 5cm (2in) in size.

2 Place the petals on the foam pad and soften and enlarge the shapes using the ball tool.

3 Frill the petal edges using the bone tool, pressing fairly firmly; be sure not to overdo it, as the chocolate will tear.

4 Place each petal edge to the edge of the foam pad and frill the petal further, this time using the cocktail stick.

5 Prepare all three shapes in the same way, then stack the petals on top of each other, offsetting them and securing in place with water. Curl the petals in slightly, and, if necessary, hold in place with folded pieces of kitchen towel until firm.

6 Re-roll the remnants of chocolate to a thickness of 1mm (¹⁄₃₂in) and cut out two petal shapes.

7 Soften the edges, as in step 3.

8 Attach as before, curling the petals in further.

9 Colour the rest of the chocolate with orange dusting powder.

10 Pinch a pea-size amount of chocolate and roll into a ball, flatten and prick the surface with the cocktail stick to make the centre of the flower.

11 Roll the remaining chocolate into a short strip approximately 25 x 12.5mm (1 x ½in). Score along the strip with the scalpel, cutting through one long side to make a fringe. Attach around the edge of the flattened ball and secure to the centre of the petals.

12 Delicately dust the edges of the petals with pale pink dusting powder.

Tools & Materials

- Basic chocolate tool kit (see page 14)
- Four-petal blossom cutter or template (see page 137)
- Kitchen towel

Makes three small flowers
- 30g (1oz) white modelling chocolate
- Orange dusting powder
- Pale pink dusting powder

2 3 4 5 10 11

EASY

EASY

05 # Forget-Me-Not

Bright blue flowers with bright yellow centres, forget-me-nots are also found in shades of pink and white. A popular garden flower, perfect for a summer garden party cake.

1 Colour two-thirds of the chocolate with the bright blue dusting powder. Colour half the remaining chocolate with the yellow dusting powder. Leave the chocolate to firm up.

2 Roll out the blue chocolate between the plastic sheets to a thickness of 1mm (⅟₃₂in).

3 Cut out as many blossoms as you desire – you could make them all the same size or use two cutters/templates and make two different sizes.

4 Place the flowers on the foam pad and, using the smaller end of the bone tool, soften the petal edges and curl them.

5 Indent the centre of each flower with the pointed end of the flower veining tool.

6 Take a tiny pinch of yellow chocolate, roll into a ball and secure in the centre of the flower with water. Use the veining tool to indent the yellow centre into the flower.

7 Arrange the flowers on the cake, interspersing them with balls of white chocolate made from the remaining modelling chocolate.

Tools & Materials

- Basic chocolate tool kit (see page 14)
- Small five-petal blossom cutter

Makes 10 flowers and 10 balls
- 15g (½oz) white modelling chocolate
- Bright blue dusting powder
- Yellow dusting powder

3

4

6

7

Mimosa EASY 06

The mimosa's leaves fold up on touch and its flowers are held in clusters.

Tools & Materials

- Basic chocolate tool kit (see page 14)
- Kitchen towel
- Leaf template (see page 136)

Makes three leaves and 16 balls
- 30g (1oz) white modelling chocolate
- Yellow pollen powder
- Yellow dusting powder
- Green dusting powder

1 Colour half the chocolate with yellow dusting powder and the other half with green. Leave the chocolate to firm up.

2 Roll the yellow chocolate into around 15 balls, of several sizes.

3 Brush the balls with water, then roll them in yellow pollen powder. Leave to dry.

4 Roll out the green chocolate between the plastic sheets to a thickness of 2mm (1/16in). Cut out several elliptical shapes with the scalpel, or use the template.

5 Place on the foam pad and soften and thin the edges using the bone tool, press lightly or you will tear the chocolate. Score down the centre with the scalpel.

6 Frill the edges with the bone tool and score the leaves with the scalpel.

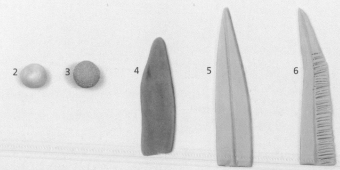

INTERMEDIATE

07 # Tulip

Striking single-stemmed flowers in bright reds, pinks, yellows and white, tulips look lovely with a simple chocolate bow (see page 71).

1 Colour one-third of the chocolate with orange dusting powder and one-third with green dusting powder, leaving the rest white. Leave the chocolate to firm up.

2 Shape a walnut-size ball of white chocolate into an egg shape. Push a cocktail stick into the broad end and stand up in the foam pad to firm up.

3 Roll out the remaining white chocolate between the plastic sheets to a thickness of 2–3mm (1/16–1/8in), then cut four petals using the rose petal cutter. Place on the foam pad.

4 Soften the chocolate and enlarge slightly using the ball tool. Work around the edge of the petal shapes, softening and thinning.

5 Draw the ball tool up each shape, curling the edges of two of the petals inward to give a slightly curved shape. Do the opposite on the other two petals, curving them outward slightly. Run the cocktail stick over these two petals to texture and grain them slightly.

6 Wrap two petals around the central shape, securing with water. Allow the petals to curve inward, and smooth the petals to the side with your fingers, making a neat and elegant shape.

7 Attach the final two petals in the same way using water, allowing them to curl out at the top. Smooth the petals down the sides and neaten underneath the shape, running the cocktail stick over the edges if necessary to continue the graining effect. Leave to firm up. Remove the cocktail stick.

8 There is enough chocolate here for two flowers, so follow the same procedure to make an orange tulip.

9 Roll a hazelnut-size ball of green chocolate into a sausage and thread onto a strand of dried spaghetti approximately 5cm (2in) long, leaving 1cm (3/8in) uncovered. Dampen the hole in the tulip base with a dot of water and insert the bare spaghetti until the green stem butts up against the tulip head.

10 Roll the remaining green chocolate between the plastic sheets and cut out five petal shapes to use as leaves.

11 Texture the leaves with the flower veining tool, drawing it up the centre of the shape then at intervals to create leaf veins. Carefully attach to the stem of the tulip with water, holding them in place until they firm up or supporting them with the kitchen towel.

Tools & Materials

- Basic chocolate tool kit, minus bone tool (see page 14)
- Large rose petal cutter or template (see page 136)
- Dried spaghetti
- Kitchen towel

Makes two flowers
- 75g (2½oz) white modelling chocolate
- Orange dusting powder
- Green dusting powder

2   3   4   6   7   9   9   11

Tools & Materials

- Basic chocolate tool kit (see page 14)
- Ball tool
- Medium chrysanthemum flower cutter
- Kitchen towel
- Cocktail stick

Makes five to seven flowers
- 30g (1oz) white modelling chocolate
- Purple dusting powder
- Yellow dusting

EASY
08 Michaelmas Daisy

A simple bloom, elegantly presented against a pale buttercream backdrop.

1 Colour three-quarters of the chocolate with purple dusting powder and the remaining quarter with the yellow. Leave the chocolate to firm up.

2 Roll out the purple chocolate between the plastic sheets to a thickness of 2–3mm (1/16–1/8in), and cut two shapes with the chrysanthemum cutter. Place on the foam pad.

3 Soften the shapes and thin slightly using the ball tool, then do the same with the bone tool, softening further and thinning more. Curl the petals up slightly too, drawing the tool from tip to centre.

4 Attach one shape to the other, offsetting the petals between each other slightly and securing in place with water.

5 Shape a pinch of the yellow chocolate into a ball that fills the centre of the flower – it should reach the base of the petals so that they look as if they are sprouting out of the yellow centre.

6 Flatten the balls, dampen with water and press into yellow dusting powder to give a 'pollen' effect. Alternatively, prick over the whole of the centre with the cocktail stick or the pointed end of the flower veining tool, or use a flower mould (see page 28) to texture.

7 Secure in the centre of the flower using water.

8 Leave the petals to firm up in a slightly curved position – this is best achieved by rolling up the kitchen towel tightly to make a strip and coiling it around into a ring. Tuck this under the petals, with the centre of the flower over the centre of the ring, and allow the petals to firm up before moving.

2

3

3
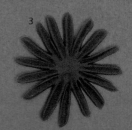

5

6

Tools & Materials
- Basic chocolate tool kit (see page 14)
- Primrose flower cutter
- Small bowl and saucer

Makes 10 flowers
- 30g (1oz) white modelling chocolate
- Yellow dusting powder
- Orange dusting powder
- Cocoa butter shavings

Primrose

INTERMEDIATE 09

The primrose is a colourful flower, found in woodland and around streams – a sign of spring.

1 Colour the modelling chocolate with yellow dusting powder, blend well and leave to firm.

2 Roll out the chocolate between the plastic sheets to a thickness of 2–3mm (¹⁄₁₆–⅛in), then cut out the required number of flower shapes.

3 Place the flowers on the foam pad and soften with the bone tool, enlarging the flower slightly, then work the ends of each petal to thin and frill just a little.

4 Indent the centre with the pointed end of the flower veining tool.

5 Shave a few curls of cocoa butter onto the saucer and place over the small bowl filled with boiling water to melt. Mix in a few grains of orange dusting powder to make a paint.

6 Paint the centre of the flowers with the paint.

1

3

6

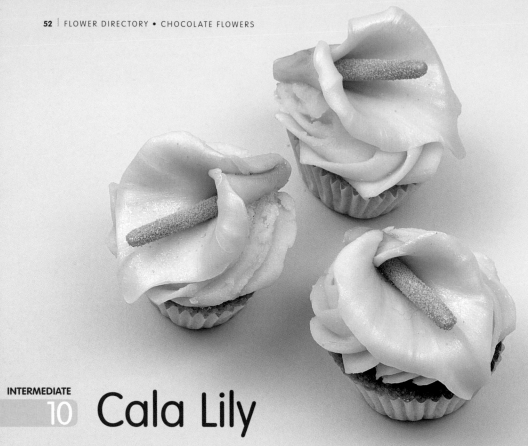

Tools & Materials
- Basic chocolate tool kit (see page 14)
- Medium cala lily cutter or template (see page 136)
- Kitchen towel

Makes three flowers
- 30g (1oz) white modelling chocolate
- Yellow dusting powder
- White dusting powder
- Green dusting powder
- Yellow pollen powder
- Sparkle dusting powder

INTERMEDIATE

10 Cala Lily

An elegant wedding flower, signifying purity and beauty.

1 Take a hazelnut-size pinch of white modelling chocolate, colour with yellow dusting powder and roll it into a sausage shape. Push a cocktail stick through the shape to make the central stamen.

2 Paint the stamen with water and cover with yellow pollen powder. Leave to firm up.

3 Colour the remaining modelling chocolate with white dusting powder, to make the chocolate a little whiter. Leave the chocolate to firm up.

4 Roll out the chocolate between the plastic sheets to a thickness of 3mm (⅛in), then cut out the lily petal using a cutter or a template.

5 Place on the foam pad. Using the flower veining tool, soften and thin the edge of the petal, working all the way around. Take care not to press too firmly or you will tear the chocolate.

6 Curl the edges of the petal back with your fingers.

7 Wrap around the yellow stamen, securing in place with water. Allow the sides of the petal to overlap, further securing the petal in position, then open up the flower.

8 Dust the stem of the lily with the green dusting powder to give the impression of the stem.

9 Dust the flower with the sparkle dusting powder and support on rolled-up kitchen towel until firm.

10 When the flower is dry, carefully twist and pull the cocktail stick out, then position the flower on the cake.

Tools & Materials

- Basic chocolate tool kit, minus flower veining tool (see page 14)
- Anthurium flower cutter or template (see page 137)
- Anthurium flower veiner
- Kitchen towel

Makes one flower
- 30g (1oz) white modelling chocolate
- Yellow dusting powder
- Red dusting powder
- Yellow pollen powder

Anthurium

EASY 11

A dramatic flower from the tropics, chocolate gives the perfect waxy appearance!

1 Colour a pea-size ball of chocolate with yellow dusting powder and the remainder with red dusting powder. Leave the chocolate to firm up.

2 Roll out the red chocolate between the plastic sheets to a thickness of 2–3mm (1/16–1/8in).

3 Cut out the anthurium shape with either a cutter or a template.

4 Place on the foam pad, running the bone tool around the edges to soften and thin the petal.

5 If you have an anthurium flower veiner, use it now – if not, use the bone tool, pressing the tool several times across the surface of the flower to give the distinctive appearance.

6 Roll up the kitchen towel tightly to make a strip and coil it around into a ring. Tuck this under the flower, with the centre of the flower over the centre of the ring, and leave to firm up.

7 Roll the yellow chocolate into a sausage shape and insert a cocktail stick to assist in maintaining the shape.

8 Paint water over the stamen and roll it in yellow pollen powder.

9 Wrap the anthurium flower around the base of the stamen and support on the rolled-up kitchen towel until firm.

10 Carefully twist and pull the cocktail stick out, then position the flower on the cake.

4

5

7   8

INTERMEDIATE

12 Anemone

A bold spring flower, the anemone appears in an array of colours and has a strong black centre.

1 Colour three-quarters of the modelling chocolate with the purple dusting powder. Leave the chocolate to firm up.

2 Roll out the purple chocolate between the plastic sheets to a thickness of 3mm (⅛in). Using a five-petal blossom cutter or a template, cut out two petal blossom shapes.

3 Place on the foam pad and soften the flower using the bone tool.

4 Run the bone tool around the edge of all the petals, thinning the edge and frilling slightly.

5 Place one flower on top of the other, offsetting the petals, and secure with water. Roll up the kitchen towel tightly and coil it around into a ring. Leave the petals to firm up in a curved position by tucking the ring under the petals, with the flower over the centre of the ring.

6 Colour the remaining chocolate with the black dusting powder.

7 Roll the black chocolate out between the plastic sheets to a thickness of 2mm (¹⁄₁₆in). Cut a strip approximately 3 x 1cm (1½ x ½in).

8 Make little cuts down one side of the strip with the scalpel to make a fringe effect.

9 Using the black remnants, make a ball of chocolate, flatten, then prick with either a cocktail stick or a flower veining tool to texture.

10 Wrap the fringe around the black flower centre, using water to secure. Position in the centre of the flower, securing with water.

Tools & Materials

- Basic chocolate tool kit, minus bone tool (see page 14)
- Celstick
- Jasmine cutter
- General leaf cutter or template (see page 136)

Makes six flowers and three leaves
- 30g (1oz) white modelling chocolate
- Green dusting powder
- Pink dusting powder
- Silver snowflake dusting powder

Jasmine

INTERMEDIATE

13

A fragrant flower that grows outside in southern Europe, and a perfect filler flower for cake arrangements.

1 Take two-thirds of the of modelling chocolate, divide into six equal portions and roll and pinch each one up like a Mexican hat (see page 24), but pinched thinly.

2 Roll the flat part of the flower with the Celstick to thin, then thread the cutter over the raised centre and cut out the flower.

3 Hold the flower in your hand and indent the centre with the flower veining tool, then draw the tool up from the centre to part way up each petal, indenting the flower as you go and making the centre larger.

4 Leave the flower to dry upside down on the trumpet section. Repeat steps 2–4 to make five more flowers.

5 Colour the remaining modelling chocolate with green dusting powder and roll out to a thickness of 2mm (¹⁄₁₆in) between the plastic sheets. Cut out two leaf shapes.

6 Accentuate the centre and base of the flower with pink dusting powder. Dust with silver snowflake dusting powder.

7 Place the leaf shape on the foam pad, soften the edges using the ball tool, then score the leaf with the flower veining tool to texture. Dust with green dusting powder to further naturalize the leaf, as seen in the image above.

2   3

EASY

14 # Camellia

The camellia has glossy, dark green leaves and large flowers made up of intricately arranged petals. This one uses red dusting powder, but you could make a camellia in white, shading through the pinks to red.

1 Colour 7g (¼oz) of the modelling chocolate with the green dusting powder and the remainder with the red dusting powder. Leave the chocolate to firm up.

2 Roll the red chocolate between the plastic sheets to a thickness of 2–3mm (¹⁄₁₆–⅛in), then cut out one extra-large, two large, three medium and three small five-petal shapes. Place them all on the foam pad.

3 Pinch together a pea-size amount of red chocolate to make a central ball for the centre of the flower.

4 Soften each petal with the bone tool. Run the tool around the edge of the petals, thinning and slightly frilling.

5 Move each of the five petals in turn to the edge of the foam pad and, using the cocktail stick, soften the chocolate, allowing the stick to texture the petals slightly.

6 Curl the edges of the petals with the bone tool.

7 Work all the blossoms in the same way.

8 Take the three smallest blossoms, place the ball of chocolate in the centre of one and secure in place with water. Curl the petals around the ball and sit it onto the second and third of the smallest petals, offsetting the petals and curling them up around the ball too to make the centre of the camellia.

9 Continue with the medium, large and extra-large blossom shapes, adding them in size order, offsetting the petals as you work.

10 Curl the petals slightly on the larger blossoms, to give a depth to the flower.

11 Roll out the green chocolate between the plastic sheets, cut out two leaves using the leaf cutter and place on the foam pad.

12 Soften the edges of the leaves with the bone tool. Using the flower veining tool, draw the pointed end down each leaf shape to texture the central stem, following with the rest of the leaf, or, alternatively, use the leaf veiner. Dust with silver snowflake dusting powder, if desired.

Tools & Materials

- Basic chocolate tool kit (see page 14)
- Five-petal blossom cutters (small, medium, large and extra large)
- Rose leaf cutter
- Rose leaf veiner (optional)

Makes one flower and two leaves
- 45g (1½oz) white modelling chocolate
- Red dusting powder
- Green dusting powder
- Silver snowflake dusting powder (optional)

Simplified camellias on afternoon cupcakes, perfect decorations in shades of pink and white.

Tools & Materials

- Basic chocolate tool kit (see page 14)
- Celstick
- Circle cutter 4.5cm (1¾in) in diameter or template (see page 137)
- 5–7 stamens per flower (small white cotton)
- Small bowl and saucer

Makes three flowers
- 30g (1oz) white modelling chocolate
- White dusting powder
- Pink dusting powder
- Yellow dusting powder
- White pollen powder
- Cocoa butter shavings

Inedible stamens
For edible stamens, see page 29

ADVANCED

15 Bindweed

Bindweed modelled in subtle shades of pink. There is a striped version of this flower, morning glory, that's also fun to make.

1 Colour the chocolate with white dusting powder and leave to firm up.

2 Pinch out a hazelnut-size piece of chocolate and roll into a ball, making it smooth and shiny. Then pinch one side of the ball, to make a Mexican hat shape (see page 24).

3 Flatten the brim of the Mexican hat section. Use the side of the Celstick to roll this flat, working all the way around.

4 Thread the circle cutter over the raised centre, and cut out a circle again.

5 Continue thinning out the flat area with a Celstick, and cut off the excess again.

6 Turn the flower over and, holding it in your hand, use the flower veining tool to indent the centre, then use the Celstick to thin the flower out to make it look like the inside of a trumpet –

or use a cocktail stick if you prefer. Work quickly, as the chocolate will melt.

7 Curl back the edge of the trumpet, then turn the flower upside down on the trumpet section and leave to firm up. This will further curl the edge of the flower.

8 Take five to seven stamens and attach to a cocktail stick with a half pea-size ball of modelling chocolate.

9 Dust the stamens with white pollen powder.

10 Push the cocktail stick through the centre of the trumpet and out through the point, pinching the chocolate around the stamens.

11 Stand the flower up and support it if necessary and leave to firm up.

12 Pour boiling water into the small bowl and place the saucer on top. Shave

a few curls of cocoa butter onto the saucer and add enough pink dusting powder to make the desired shade. Paint the edges of the flower, as shown above.

13 Dust the centre of the flower with the yellow dusting powder. When dry, after 24 hours, pull out the cocktail stick before placing the flower on the cake surface.

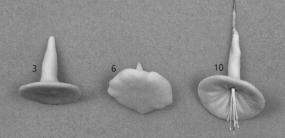

Tools & Materials

- Basic chocolate tool kit (see page 14)
- Celstick
- Periwinkle flower cutter
- Periwinkle leaf cutter
- 5 stamens (small white cotton)

Makes three flowers and three leaves
- 30g (1oz) white modelling chocolate
- Pale lilac dusting powder
- Green dusting powder
- Yellow pollen powder

Inedible stamens
For edible stamens, see page 29

Periwinkle

The periwinkle has striking stellar-blue flowers, a colour that can be recreated with pale lilac dusting powder.

1 Colour all but 3.5g (⅛oz) of the chocolate with thr pale lilac dusting powder. Colour the remaining chocolate green for the leaf. Leave to firm up.

2 Take a hazelnut-size pinch of the chocolate and roll into a smooth ball. Pinch one side of the ball, twisting and pulling to make a Mexican hat shape (see page 24).

3 Flatten the brim of the Mexican hat section. Use the side of the Celstick to roll this flat, working all the way around.

4 Thread the periwinkle cutter over the pulled-up section in the centre and cut out a periwinkle shape.

5 Continue thinning out the flat area with a Celstick or cocktail stick. Run the cocktail stick over the petals to thin them slightly and texture them. Cut off the excess again.

6 Turn the flower over. Holding it in your hand, use the flower veining tool to indent the centre, then use the Celstick to thin out the petals to make it look like the inside of a trumpet. Work quickly, as the chocolate will melt.

7 Curl back the edge of the trumpet. Turn the flower upside down on the trumpet section and leave it to firm up. This will further curl the edge of the flower.

8 Take five stamens and attach to a cocktail stick with a half pea-size ball of modelling chocolate.

9 Dust the stamens with pollen powder.

10 Push the cocktail stick through the centre of the trumpet and out through the point, pinching the chocolate to the stamens.

11 Stand the flower up and support it if necessary. Leave to firm up.

12 Dust the flower with lilac dusting powder to accentuate the colour and give depth to the colouring. When dry, after 24 hours, pull out the cocktail stick.

13 Roll out the green chocolate between the plastic sheets to a thickness of 2–3mm (1⁄16–⅛in). Cut out the leaf, using the cutter. Place the leaf on the foam pad, and texture with the flower veining tool.

ADVANCED
17

Water Lily

This is a striking flower that lasts only a few days, quickly replaced with a new flower – and there are so many colours to choose from!

1 Colour three-quarters of the chocolate with pink dusting powder. Split the remaining chocolate in half and use the dusting powders to colour half yellow and half green. Leave to firm up. Roll the pink chocolate between the plastic sheets to a thickness of 3mm (⅛in). Cut out 12 petal shapes in total, then cut off their bases to give a flattened end. On the foam pad, soften the petal edges with the ball tool.

2 Using the pointed end of the flower veining tool, vein each petal of the blossom, press firmly up the centre, and pull the chocolate a little to shape the petal into an oval. Pinch the point of the petal slightly to exaggerate the shape.

3 Curl the petal up with the bone tool, then place on rolled-up kitchen towel to maintain the shape of the petals while they firm up. Do the same with the second and subsequent petal shapes.

4 Place one petal on top of another, offsetting the petals in rows, securing with water and pressing gently together. Support with rolled kitchen towel until the petals are holding themselves; this will take approximately two or three hours.

5 Take half of the yellow chocolate. Roll into a ball, flatten and prick several times with the cocktail stick to make the centre of the flower. Dust with pollen powder if desired.

6 Roll the remaining yellow chocolate into a strip approximately 25 x 12.5mm (1 x ½in). Score along one long side of the strip with the scalpel to make a fringe. Attach around the edge of the flattened ball and secure to the centre of the flower with water.

7 Roll out the green chocolate between plastic sheets to a thickness of 3mm (⅛in). Cut out a circle shape with a circle cutter or freehand. Use the flower veining tool to indent the circle edge, as in the image.

8 Use the same tool to texture the leaf with veins.

Tools & Materials

- Basic chocolate tool kit (see page 14)
- Rose petal cutter, 2.5–3cm (1–1¼in) or template (see page 136)
- Kitchen towel
- Circle cutter (optional)

Makes one flower and one leaf
- 30g (1oz) white modelling chocolate
- Pink dusting powder
- Yellow dusting powder
- Green dusting powder
- Yellow pollen powder (optional)

1

1

2

5

6

6

7

8

Striking water
lilies show their
elegant petals.

EASY
18 Ivy Wreath

Ivy leaves are the perfect 'filler' leaf for many flower arrangements. Here they are shown in a seasonal wreath.

1 Colour 7g (¼oz) of the chocolate green and 14g (⅔oz) red. Colour the rest of the chocolate yellow.

2 Roll the green chocolate out between the plastic sheets to a thickness of 2–3mm (¹⁄₁₆–⅛in).

3 Cut out the leaves either with a cutter or a template, then place them on the foam pad.

4 Soften the edges with the bone tool.

5 Place the leaf on the leaf veiner and emboss the surface to make it

look more realistic. If you don't have an ivy leaf veiner, use the pointed end of the flower veining tool to vein the leaves by hand.

6 Make the little flowers from red and yellow chocolate by following the forget-me-not instructions on page 46.

Make as many berries from red chocolate as desired.

7 Position the leaves onto the cake or cupcake along with the flowers and berries, and secure in place with water.

Tools & Materials

- Basic chocolate tool kit (see page 14)
- Ivy leaf cutter or template (see page 137)
- Ivy leaf veiner

Makes eight leaves, 20 flowers and 20 berries
- 30g (1oz) white modelling chocolate
- Green dusting powder
- Red dusting powder
- Yellow dusting powder

For the flower, see the forget-me-not on page 46.

Pansy

They come in so many different shades, make one in your favorite colour!

Tools & Materials

- Basic chocolate tool kit, minus flower veining tool (see page 14)
- Pansy blossom flower cutter or templates (see page 139)
- Kitchen towel
- Small bowl and saucer

Makes three flowers
- 30g (1oz) white modelling chocolate
- Lilac dusting powder
- Yellow dusting powder
- Cocoa butter shavings

1 Use lilac dusting powder to colour a hazelnut-size ball of modelling chocolate. Reserve the same amount of white chocolate for the centre of the pansy. Roll the remaining white chocolate and the lilac chocolate between the plastic sheets to a thickness of 2–3mm (1/16–1/8in).

2 Cut out three small petals (one petal from the lilac chocolate and two from the white chocolate) and one large petal from the white chocolate. Place them on the foam pad.

3 Soften the edges with the bone tool, but don't press too firmly as the chocolate will tear.

4 Frill the large white petal and the lilac petal more than the other two petals.

5 Position the petals in order: the lilac petal at the back, then the two small white ones either side with their centres lined up with the lilac centre, and the largest petal on top, as per the image. Secure with water.

6 Leave to firm up on rolled-up kitchen towel. Take the remnant of white modelling chocolate, colour it yellow with the dusting powder and roll it into a ball. Position in the centre of the pansy and indent with the flower veining tool.

7 Place shavings of cocoa butter on the saucer, then place over the small bowl with boiling water, to allow it to melt.

8 Make purple and yellow paints with the melted cocoa butter and dusting powders. Paint the petals of the pansy, following the colours in the photo. .

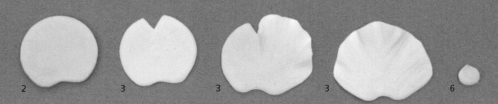

2   3   3   3   6

Marzipan
Flowers

Rose

This is the easiest rose to make; by wrapping the marzipan around itself, the stylized flower appears.

Tools & Materials

- Basic marzipan tool kit (see page 14)
- Pizza cutter
- Textured rolling pin (optional)

Makes one large and five small flowers, and 12 balls
- 30g (1oz) natural-coloured marzipan
- Red dusting powder

1 Colour the marzipan with the red dusting powder, and leave the marzipan to firm up.

2 Roll the marzipan out between the plastic sheets to a thickness of 2–3mm (1/16–1/8in). It is not easy to manipulate the marzipan if it is too thin.

3 Cut the marzipan into rectangular strips approximately 2.5 x 10cm (1 x 4in).

4 Texture the strip using the textured rolling pin, if desired.

5 Fold the strip gently in half along its length.

6 Roll the strip up, coiling it up quite tightly to start with to get a good centre to the rose, then allow the coiling to become looser as you go along, creating the outer petals of the flower.

7 If you want smaller flowers, stop coiling at the desired point and cut away the excess marzipan.

INTERMEDIATE

21 Lily

This is a flower that needs some support while drying, since it is unwired. It is a perfect flower for a birthday cake.

1 Colour the marzipan with the yellow dusting powder and leave the marzipan to firm up.

2 Roll the marzipan between the plastic sheets to a thickness of 2–3mm (¹⁄₁₆–⅛in), then cut out three broad and three narrow petals using the cutters or templates. Place each petal on the foam pad.

3 Use the bone tool to soften around the edges of each petal, then use the lily petal veiner to texture the petals. If you do not have a petal veiner available, use the flower veining tool instead.

4 Curl the petals and support with rolled-up pieces of kitchen towel. Leave to firm up until the petals hold their own shape.

5 Attach the cotton stamens loosely to the cocktail stick with floral tape; alternatively, use a tiny strip of marzipan to secure the stamens in place. Wrap the floral tape tightly around the cocktail stick below the stamens, as you will be removing this later.

6 Dust the stamens with pollen powder to give the pollen effect.

7 Secure the petals around the stamen centre with water. Attach the broad petals first, then the narrow ones.

8 Leave the flower to dry and set, supported on rolled-up kitchen towel, for approximately 48 hours. Twist the cocktail stick while carefully holding the flower, removing the cocktail stick and floral tape, but leaving the stamens in place.

Tools & Materials

- Basic marzipan tool kit (see page 14)
- Lily petal cutter or template (see page 136)
- Lily petal veiner
- Cotton stamens (six or seven per flower)
- Floral tape
- Rolled-up kitchen towel

Makes one flower
- 45g (1½oz) natural-coloured marzipan
- Yellow dusting powder
- Yellow pollen powder

Inedible stamens
For edible stamens, see page 29

1   2   5   6   7

Lily (instructions
opposite) and coiled
fantasy flower
in flower paste
(see page 100).

Tools & Materials
- Basic marzipan tool kit, minus flower veining tool (see page 14)
- Orchid cutting set
- Ball tool
- Orchid veiner
- Rolled-up kitchen towel

Makes one flower and one leaf
- 30g (1oz) natural-coloured marzipan
- Pink dusting powder
- Red dusting powder
- Green dusting powder
- Dot of royal icing to secure the petals

ADVANCED

22 Orchid

The orchid is a delicate flower, so try to roll the marzipan as thinly as you can and support the petals while drying. The marzipan will hold its shape if it is dried for long enough.

1 Colour three-quarters of the marzipan with pink dusting powder. Leave to firm.

2 Roll the pink marzipan between the plastic sheets to a thickness of 2mm (1/16in), then cut out three narrow petals, two larger petals and the central section. Place on the foam pad.

3 Soften the edges of the five petals using the bone tool.

4 Frill the petals' edges with the cocktail stick.

5 Soften the central part of the petals with the bone tool. Rub the tool over the whole shape, enlarging it slightly and gently curling the parts of the shape inward.

6 Use the ball tool to curl the central throat of the orchid, curl the two side elements inward and the lower bulbous section upward.

7 Use the orchid veiner to add texture to each of the petals. Support the petals with rolled-up kitchen towel.

8 Position the three smaller petals on the cake or cupcake as shown above and secure with a dot of royal icing. Position the two large semicircular petals on top, at either side of the centre of the flower, securing as before.

9 Position the curled-up orchid throat on the centre of the flower, securing as before. Shade the petals with pink and red dusting powder.

10 Take a pinch of pink marzipan and roll it into a small teardrop that will fit inside the centre of the flower. Indent down each side of the teardrop and attach to the centre of the flower by the pointed end.

11 Colour the remaining marzipan with green dusting powder. Allow the marzipan to firm up again. Roll out between the plastic sheets to a thickness of 3mm (1/8in). Cut out a rough oval shape, texture with the flower veining tool and attach behind the flower. Support with a rolled-up kitchen towel until firm, for approximately two or three hours.

2 2 2 3 3 4  6 10 10 11

Tools & Materials

- Basic marzipan tool kit (see page 14)
- Poinsettia cutters or templates (see page 139)
- Flower veining tool
- Rolled-up kitchen towel

Makes one flower
- 30g (1oz) natural-coloured marzipan
- Red dusting powder

Poinsettia

EASY
23

The poinsettia's striking scarlet leaves, here made in marzipan, are perfect for decorating Christmas cakes.

1 Colour two-thirds of marzipan red and the remaining third pink. Blend until even, and leave to firm up.

2 Roll out the red marzipan between the plastic sheets to a thickness of 2–3mm (1/16–1/8in).

3 Cut out the poinsettia bracts using the cutters or templates and a scalpel. Several sizes of bract are required, from very small up to large and four or five of each. Place on the foam pad.

4 Soften the edges of the bracts with the bone tool.

5 Run the flower veining tool up the centre of the bracts to texture – you could use a poinsettia veiner, if available.

6 Attach the bracts in rosettes to the top of the cake or cupcake, using dots of water – start with the large bracts around the outside, working inward, overlaying the bracts with smaller ones.

7 Finish with tiny pink balls of marzipan in the centre, using water to secure in place.

EASY
24 Holly and Berries

Another perfect decoration for a Christmas cake, easy to make and effective when teamed up with the poinsettia and mistletoe.

1 Colour a hazelnut-size ball of marzipan with red dusting powder, blend until even and leave to firm up. Colour the remaining marzipan with green dusting powder.

2 Roll the green marzipan out between the plastic sheets to a thickness of 2–3mm (1/16–1/8in), then cut out seven to nine leaf shapes using either the cutter or a template.

3 Place on the foam pad and soften around the edges with the bone tool.

4 Use the holly leaf veiner to texture the leaf, or use the flower veining tool if you don't have a holly leaf veiner available.

5 Position the leaves on the cake or cupcake and secure with water.

6 Roll the red marzipan into small balls for the berries – three for the base of each leaf – and secure in the same way.

Tools & Materials
- Basic marzipan tool kit (see page 14)
- Holly leaf cutter or template (see page 139)
- Holly leaf veiner (optional)

Makes seven leaves and 24 berries
- 30g (1oz) natural-coloured marzipan
- Red dusting powder
- Green dusting powder

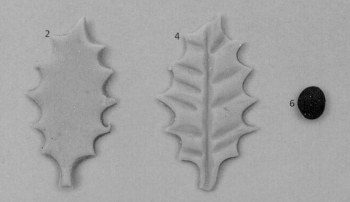

Mistletoe EASY 25

Easy to make and teams well with the other flowers used to decorate Christmas cakes.

Tools & Materials

- Basic marzipan tool kit (see page 14)
- General leaf cutter or template (see page 136)
- General leaf veiner

Makes seven leaves, 12–15 berries and one bow

- 45g (1½oz) natural-coloured marzipan
- White dusting powder (or icing sugar)
- Green dusting powder
- Red dusting powder

1 Colour 21g (¾oz) of the marzipan with the green dusting powder, 14g (½oz) of the marzipan with the white dusting powder or icing sugar and 7g (¼oz) with the red dusting powder. Leave to firm up.

2 Roll the green marzipan between the plastic sheets to a thickness of 3mm (⅛in), then cut out seven leaves. Place on the foam pad.

3 Use the bone tool to soften around the edges of the leaves, elongating them. Using the flower veining tool or general leaf veiner, vein each leaf.

4 Position the leaves on the cupcake or cake and secure with water.

5 Shape the white marzipan into 12–15 balls for the berries of the mistletoe and attach in the same way.

6 Roll the red marzipan between plastic sheets to a thickness of 2–3mm (1/16–⅛in). Cut two rectangular strips approximately 1 x 6cm (⅜ x 2¼in). Cut one strip into two pieces, and cut a triangle out of one end of each piece for the ribbon ends. Fold the other rectangle centrally to form the bow.

7 Position the bow on the cake, with the two ribbon tails underneath, and secure in place with water. Use the remnants of red marzipan to make the centre of the bow: roll out the marzipan as before, cutting a shorter rectangle but still 1cm (⅜in) in width. Secure over the centre of the bow with water.

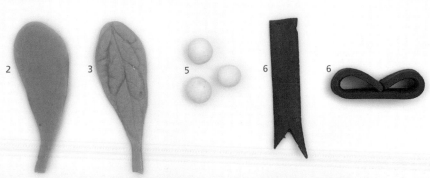

2　　3　　5　　6　　6

EASY
26 Bramble

This is a favourite of mine. The flowers are made using flower paste, since natural marzipan is a yellow colour and I wanted a flower with a white base.

1 Colour two-thirds of the marzipan with the purple dusting powder, and leave to firm up. Colour the remaining marzipan with the green dusting powder.

2 Shape a hazelnut-size ball of the purple marzipan into a cone shape, then insert a cocktail stick through the flat base. You need one of these per bramble.

3 Make the remaining purple marzipan into tiny balls, attaching them to the cone with water. Press them together, working from the top to the base.

4 Roll the green marzipan between the plastic sheets to a thickness of 2–3mm (¹⁄₁₆–⅛in), then cut out three to five leaves for each cupcake.

5 Place the leaves on the foam pad and soften around the edges with the bone tool.

6 Texture the leaves with the veiner or use the flower veining tool to vein by hand.

7 Remove the cocktail stick from the base of the bramble and attach it to the cake or cupcake with water.

8 The flower is made from flower paste. Follow the instructions for the cherry blossom (see page 106) but use yellow pollen powder for the pollen.

Tools & Materials
- Basic marzipan tool kit (see page 14)
- Rose leaf cutter or template (see page 136)
- Rose leaf veiner

Makes two berries and five leaves
- 45g (1½oz) natural-coloured marzipan
- Purple dusting powder
- Green dusting powder
- Yellow pollen powder

For the flower, see page 106

Inedible stamens
For edible stamens, see page 29

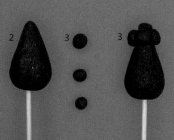

These pretty bramble cupcakes would be perfect for an autumn tea party.

EASY
27 Pine Cone

This is easy if you have a mould and a little more challenging if you are making the pine cone freehand.

1 Colour all of the marzipan with the brown dusting powder, blend until even and leave to firm up. Take a hazelnut-size piece and press it firmly into the mould. Scrape off any excess from the top, making the marzipan flush with the top of the mould.

2 Turn the mould over and tap until the shaped marzipan drops out cleanly. Make more pine cones using the same method.

3 If you don't have a mould available, shape the marzipan into an oval, then snip the side of the oval at regular intervals with a pair of scissors to create a spiked effect.

4 Shape the remnants of marzipan into a sausage shape, approximately 2.5 x 0.5cm (1 x ¼in) to represent the stalk of the pine cones.

Tools & Materials
- Pine cone mould
- Scissors (optional)

Makes three cones
- 45g (1½oz) natural-coloured marzipan
- Brown dusting powder

1

3

4

Hellebore

Hellebores are lovely, subtle flowers. Make them in a range of colours – greens, purples, pinks and natural cream.

Tools & Materials

- Basic marzipan tool kit (see page 14)
- Large five-petal blossom cutter or template (see page 137)
- Cotton stamens (15 per flower)

Makes three flowers
- 30g (1oz) natural-coloured marzipan
- Purple dusting powder
- Yellow dusting powder
- Yellow pollen powder (optional)

Inedible stamens
For edible stamens, see page 29

1 Colour two-thirds of the marzipan with purple dusting powder, blend until even and leave to firm up.

2 Roll the marzipan out between plastic sheets to a thickness of 2–3mm ($\frac{1}{16}$–$\frac{1}{8}$in).

3 Cut out the blossom and place on the foam pad.

4 Soften the petal edges with the bone tool. Don't press too firmly, otherwise you will tear the marzipan. Curl the edges inward to a slight point.

5 Draw the bone tool from the edge of the petal to the centre, to curl the marzipan upward and inward.

6 Colour the remaining marzipan with the yellow dusting powder. Roll into a ball, flatten and texture with the cocktail stick to represent the centre of the flower.

7 Dust the stamens with yellow pollen powder and insert them around the sides of the flower centre.

8 Secure the flower centre to the petal using water.

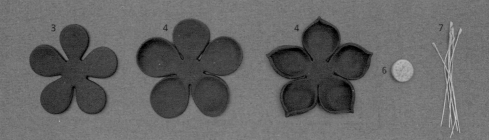

Flower Paste Flowers

Tools & Materials
- Basic flower paste tool kit (see page 14)
- 0.5mm (24-gauge) wire
- Singapore orchid cutter kit
- Bone tool
- Floral tape (Nile green)
- Rolled-up kitchen towel
- Posy pick

Makes one flower
- 30g (1oz) flower paste
- Pink dusting powder
- Green dusting powder
- Silver snowflake dusting powder

Inedible flower

Singapore Orchid

ADVANCED
29

The Singapore orchid is a delicate, elegant flower – not the easiest to make, but well worth the effort. The beautiful shading on the petals gives it a very realistic appearance.

1 Shape the column of the flower using the mould provided in the cutter kit. Insert a 0.5mm (24-gauge) wire up the centre of the column, then leave to dry.

2 Roll out a small amount of paste and cut out the broad throat petal using the cutter. Press the shape into the cutter as you cut to texture the paste.

3 Tap the shape out of the cutter, insert a 0.5mm (24-gauge) wire up the centre, place on the foam pad and soften the edges slightly with the bone tool.

4 Dampen the base of the petal and wrap it around the column, with the column facing in towards the petal. Tape the wires together using floral tape.

5 When dry, cut out, texture and soften the triple petal shape and two single petals in the same way.

6 Place the two single petals on top of the triple petal shape, as shown below, and secure in place with a dot of water.

7 Take the throat section and place the base against the point where the petals meet. Dampen with water then pinch the petals around the base of the throat. Allow the lower section of the triple petal to stick out behind, then pinch it together.

8 Place on the foam pad, using a rolled-up kitchen towel to support it.

9 Dust the petals with the pink and green dusting powder, then finish with a dusting of silver snowflake powder. Insert the posy pick into the cake, then insert the flower into this.

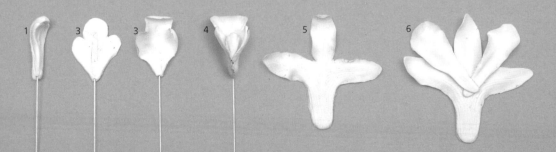

30 Rose

The rose is the typical English flower that can be found in almost any colour – the flower of weddings, birthdays and afternoon tea. Looking at it, you can almost smell its aroma!

1 Colour two-thirds of the paste with pink paste colour. Take a hazelnut-size pinch of pink paste, shape into a cone and push onto the end of a cocktail stick.

2 Roll out the remaining pink paste to a thickness of 1mm (¹⁄₃₂in) and cut out five petals.

3 Place the petals on the foam pad and soften around the edges of two petals with the bone tool – rub the whole petal with the tool to soften the rest of the petal.

4 Take the cocktail stick and run it lightly around the edge of the petals.

5 Dampen the cone and wrap the two petals around the cone, overlapping on both sides.

6 Prepare the other three petals in the same way and attach to the cone, interlocking each petal with the previous to give a coil effect to the centre of the flower. Curl the edges of the petals more using the cocktail stick to make them more frilly.

7 Continue preparing petals – five are required for the next row and seven for the row after – interlocking the petals as you attach them to the flower.

8 Leave the flower to dry for five minutes after you have added each row of petals – this makes it easier, as the previous row won't move about. It is a good idea to make several flowers at once, so by the time you get back to the first it is dry enough to work on.

9 For the leaf, colour the remaining paste with green paste colour. Cut out the general leaf shape and vein using the general leaf veiner.

10 Dust the flower with pink dusting powder, adding more at the centre, then finish with a dust of silver snowflake powder. Dust the leaves with the green powder.

11 Before displaying the flower, pull the cocktail stick out from the base. Position on the cake.

Tools & Materials

- Basic flower paste tool kit, minus flower veining tool (see page 14)
- Rose petal cutter
- General leaf cutter or bramble leaf template (see page 138)
- General leaf veiner
- Bone tool
- Cocktail stick

Makes one large flower
- 30g (1oz) flower paste
- Pink paste colour
- Green paste colour
- Pink dusting powder
- Silver snowflake dusting powder
- Green dusting powder

1   2   3   4   4   5   6   7   9   9   9   10

You could add one or more roses to your cakes or cupcakes, either with or without leaves, depending on your design requirements.

Tools & Materials

- Basic flower paste tool kit (see page 14)
- Lily cutter or template (see page 136)
- Lily petal and leaf veiner
- Bone tool
- Cocktail stick
- 0.5mm (24-gauge) wire cut into thirds
- 8 cotton stamens
- Floral tape (green)
- Posy pick

Makes one flower and three leaves
- 30g (1oz) flower paste
- Yellow paste colour
- Green paste colour
- Brown pollen powder
- Red dusting powder
- Pink dusting powder
- Silver snowflake dusting powder

Inedible flower

INTERMEDIATE

31 Starburst Lily

A very startling flower with a strong scent, the starburst lily is a definite statement flower.

1 Colour a pea-size pinch of paste with yellow paste colour and shape it into a cone. Push in a small length of 0.5mm (24-gauge) wire from the pointed end of the cone, leaving the other end flat for the stigma.

2 Brush eight stamens with water and dust with brown pollen powder, then attach to the stigma with green floral tape. Tweak the stamens into a neat position.

3 Roll out two-thirds of the white flower paste to a thickness of 1–2mm (1/32–1/16 in). Cut out three small and three large petals, using the cutters or templates and a scalpel.

4 Thread a strand of 0.5mm (24-gauge) wire through the base and three-quarters of the way up each petal. Place on the foam pad.

5 Soften around the edges of the petals, running the bone tool along the edge, thinning the paste.

Texture the petals by pressing between the lily veiner, then ruffle the edges of each petal with the bone tool.

6 Bend each petal into a natural position, pinch the base of the petal together to thin and leave upright to dry for 20 minutes, either in a petal stand or in a wine glass. Repeat for all petals.

7 Dust the petals with red dusting powder, drawing it up the petals from base to tip with the paintbrush, tailing off towards the tip.

Use the pink dusting powder either side of the red, to blend out the colour.

8 Tape the petals together, starting with the larger petals, then place the smaller ones between and behind each large one.

9 Colour the remaining paste with the green paste colour, then roll out between plastic sheets to a thickness of 1–2mm (1/32–1/16 in). Cut out the three leaves using the smaller of the lily petal cutters or templates.

10 Insert a strand of 0.5mm (24-gauge) wire into the leaves, as for the petals.

11 Soften the edges of the leaves with the bone tool. Texture the leaf using the flower veining tool.

12 Use strands of floral tape to wire the leaves behind the flower head. Dust with silver snowflake dusting powder if desired. Insert the posy pick into the cake, then insert the flower into this.

1 1 2 2 4 5 8 5 8 8 10 11

Tools & Materials

- Basic flower paste tool kit (see page 14)
- Large five-petal daisy cutter
- Small six-petal daisy cutter
- Bone tool
- Celstick
- Cocktail stick (optional)

Makes six flowers
- 30g (1oz) flower paste
- Yellow pollen powder
- Green paste colour
- Green dusting powder
- Silver snowflake dusting powder (optional)

Star of Bethlehem

EASY
32

This flower is found on stalks of ten or fifteen flowers in nature, but they are so pretty and fresh, they look perfect displayed in a small group or individually on a cupcake.

1 Roll out two-thirds of the white flower paste to a thickness of 1–2mm ($\frac{1}{32}$–$\frac{1}{16}$in). Cut out a large five-petal daisy shape and place on the foam pad.

2 Soften around the edges of the daisy with the bone tool, then use the Celstick to broaden and lengthen the petals,

leaving a little texture as you work. If you prefer, you can do this with a cocktail stick.

3 Cut out a small six-petal daisy and work in the same way.

4 Draw the bone tool up each petal, curling them up together.

5 Dampen each point of the small daisy shape with a dot of water, then turn upside down into the pollen powder, allowing it to stick to the ends of each petal.

6 Position the smaller daisy in the centre of the large daisy, securing it with a dot of water.

7 Take the remaining paste and colour it with green paste colour.

8 Take a pinch of paste and roll it into a ball. Flatten slightly then use the scalpel to cut little triangles out of the ball.

9 Indent the cuts with the pointed end of the flower veining tool to neaten.

10 Position the green ball shape in the centre of the flower and secure with a dot of water.

11 Dust with silver snowflake dusting powder if desired.

ADVANCED

33 Fuchsia

Fuchsias can be made in a multitude of different colours, dangling from thin stems, almost looking as though a gust of wind would blow the delicate flowers off.

1 Cut 10cm (4in) of white floral tape and cut into three strips lengthwise. Take five to seven stamens and attach to a 0.5mm (24-gauge) wire, using the floral tape. Make sure the stamens are at different lengths, with one that stands out as the longest.

2 Paint the stamens using the red dusting powder. Allow to dry, then dust with red dusting powder. Blow off any excess.

3 Roll out a small pinch of white paste to a thickness of 1mm (1/32in), cut out one blossom and place it on the foam pad.

4 Soften the petal edges with the ball tool then, using the cocktail stick or ball tool, frill the edges lightly. Draw the ball tool up the petals, curling them inward slightly.

5 Thread the blossom down the stamen stalk, moulding and overlapping the petals around the stamens, securing the petals in place with a dot of water.

6 Allow to dry in an upturned position so that the petals stay curled around the stamens.

7 Colour 7g (1/4oz) paste with the red paste colour to create a light pink. Blend in the colour.

8 Roll the paste into a ball, then create the sepal using the Mexican hat method (see page 24).

9 Cut out a base for the fuchsia using the scalpel. It requires four sepals, so cut one at each side, like a compass.

10 Soften the edges of the cut sepals with the ball tool on the foam pad, then use the ball tool to

draw up each sepal – this will curl them back.

11 Thread the pink sepal down the stamen stalk behind the white blossom, and secure with a dot of water.

12 Colour 15g (1/2oz) of paste with the green paste colour. Thread a pea-size ball of green paste down the stamen, and secure it in place with a dot of water. Shape the ball so that it is slightly elongated and tapers onto the wire.

13 Tape the wire with thin strips of green floral tape. Dust the green paste and the tape where they join with green dusting powder to give a seamless colour.

14 Roll out 10g (1/3oz) of green paste to make the leaves. Cut out the leaves using the leaf cutter or template and scalpel.

15 Insert a strand of 0.5mm (24-gauge) wire up the centre of the leaf, then place it in the leaf veiner and press firmly. If you don't have a veiner, use the flower veining tool to create the veins by hand.

16 Tape the wire with green floral tape, then dust the wire and leaf with green dusting powder to give a natural appearance. Attach the leaf to the flower using floral tape.

17 Make one more flower and two more leaves in the same way. Dust the whole display with silver snowflake dusting powder if desired.

18 Insert the end of each stem into a posy pick; each posy pick will accommodate three stems.

Tools & Materials
- Basic flower paste tool kit (see page 14)
- Floral tape (white and green)
- Cotton stamens (five to seven per flower)
- 0.5mm (24-gauge) wire (white taped) cut into thirds
- Blossom cutter
- Celstick
- Ball tool
- Cocktail stick
- General leaf cutter or bramble leaf template (see page 138)
- General leaf veiner
- Posy pick

Makes two flowers and three leaves
- 30g (1oz) flower paste
- Red dusting powder
- Red paste colour
- Green paste colour
- Green dusting powder
- Silver snowflake dusting powder (optional)

Inedible flower

If you prefer, rather than a ball at the base of the flower, you could use a star-shaped sepal, as shown on the finished cake.

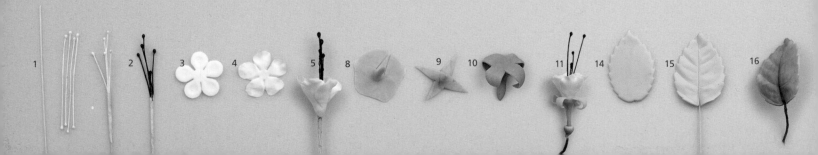

1   2   3   4   5   8   9   10   11   14   15   16

To create a stem of fuchsias, take 10cm (4in) of red floral tape and cut into three lengthwise. Use one thinner strip at a time and taking a full length of 0.5mm (24-gauge) wire, tape the flower to the wire, adding a new flower every 2cm (¾in).

Tools & Materials

- Basic flower paste tool kit (see page 14)
- 0.5mm (24-gauge) wire cut into thirds
- At least 20 black cotton stamens per flower
- Floral tape (white and Nile green)
- Celstick
- Stephanotis or jasmine or star cutter
- Ball tool
- Posy pick

Makes one spray
- 30g (1oz) flower paste
- Blue paste colour
- Green paste colour
- Green dusting powder

Inedible flower

INTERMEDIATE

34 Cornflower

A deep blue flower that looks so striking with the contrasting green leaf, which is not as complicated to make as you may think.

1 Take a strand of wire, bend over a small hook at one end and attach a stamen using white floral tape.

2 Colour 22g (¾oz) of the paste blue and the remainder green. Take a hazelnut-size ball of blue paste and create a flower using the Mexican hat method (see page 24).

3 Roll the flat part of the flower with the Celstick to thin it, then thread the cutter over the raised centre and cut out the petals.

4 Hold the flower in your hand and indent the centre with the flower veining tool, then draw the tool up from the centre to part way up each petal, indenting the flower as you go and making the centre larger.

5 Thread the hooked wire through the centre of the flower, concealing it within the flower.

6 Leave the flower to dry – either upright or hanging upside down.

7 Make the leaf by rolling out a hazelnut-size ball of green paste to a thickness of 1mm (¹⁄₃₂in), then use the scalpel to cut a rectangle of 1 x 4cm (½ x 1½in). Shape one end into an oval and the other to a point. Push a 0.5mm (24-gauge) wire three-quarters of the way down the length of the leaf.

8 Place the shape on the foam pad, softening the edges using the ball tool, then score the leaf with the flower veining tool to texture. Bend the top over slightly to give a natural appearance. Dust with the green dusting powder.

9 Make more flowers and leaves in the same way.

10 Take a central stem of wire and tape with Nile green floral tape.

11 Attach the stamens to the top of the stem with Nile green floral tape, then tape the flowers around this at intervals.

12 Pull out the stamens in the centre in a random way, then attach the leaves at the base of the flower with Nile green floral tape. Insert the posy pick into the cake, then insert the flower into this.

Tools & Materials

- Basic flower paste tool kit (see page 14)
- Daphne cutter
- Celstick
- 0.5mm (24-gauge) wire cut into thirds
- Leaf template (see page 139)
- Floral tape (Nile green)
- Bone tool
- Posy pick

Makes one spray
- 30g (1oz) flower paste
- Lilac paste colour
- Green paste colour
- Green dusting powder
- Silver snowflake dusting powder (optional)

Inedible flower

Lilac INTERMEDIATE 35

The beautiful lilac is equally pretty when made in white. The flowers are not difficult to make and the display can be as large or as small as is needed.

1 Colour three-quarters of the paste with the lilac paste colour. Roll a small pinch into a ball, then create one of the flowers using the Mexican hat method (see page 24).

2 Use the Celstick to thin the flattened part, thread the cutter over the raised centre and cut out the shape using the daphne cutter.

3 Hold the flower in your hand and use the pointed end of the flower veining tool to open up the centre of the flower.

4 Draw the tool over the petals, softening and thinning them, and use the pointed end of the tool to texture the petals.

5 Take a strand of 0.5mm (24-gauge) wire, bend a tiny hook in one end and thread it through the flower centre, pulling the little hook into the flower until it disappears. Thin the paste at the base of the flower onto the wire.

Make several lilac flowers in the same way.

6 Take another pinch of lilac paste, roll it into a ball, then thread another hooked wire into the ball. Shape the ball into a teardrop, thinning the paste to the wire.

7 Use the scalpel to indent a cross at the end of the teardrop to represent the bud petals. Make several buds.

8 Wire all the buds and flowers together, using a thin strand of green floral tape. Start with a few buds, then add in a blossom or two, giving a natural look.

9 Colour the remaining paste with the green paste colour, then cut out a leaf shape using the template and the scalpel. Insert a strand of 0.5mm (24-gauge) wire up the centre of the leaf.

10 Soften the edges of the leaf on the foam pad with the bone tool, then vein the leaf with a veiner or by hand. Dust with green dusting powder to add a natural appearance.

11 Attach the leaves to the back of the lilac spray with Nile green floral tape, as before. Dust the spray with silver snowflake dusting powder, if desired. Insert the posy pick into the cake, then insert the flower into this.

INTERMEDIATE

36 Snowdrop

The snowdrop is one of the first signs of spring. The delicate snowdrops pushing up through the snow can be all shades of green – an array of bobbing heads!

1 Take a length of 0.5mm (24-gauge) wire and create a small hook on the end.

2 Roll a pea-size ball of paste and thread it down the wire over the hook. Dampen the end of the ball and dip it into the pollen powder.

3 Roll the paste out to a thickness of 1mm (1/32in). Using the cutters, cut two trefoil shapes, one larger than the other. Place on the foam pad.

4 Soften the edges of the shapes with the ball tool, broadening and thinning the paste, then draw the tool up the shape to curl the petals.

5 Thread the smaller petal shape up the wire behind the ball and secure in place with a dot of water.

6 Repeat with the second petal shape.

7 Colour the remaining paste green.

8 Take a pea-size ball of paste, roll it into a cone.

Thread the cone down the wire to butt up against the back of the petals. Secure with water.

9 Tape the wire with Nile green floral tape, then bend over the wire approximately 1cm (1/2in) down from the head to give the snowdrop shape.

10 Take another pinch of green paste and shape it into a second cone. Attach it to the wire at the bend, using water.

11 Roll the remaining green paste to a thickness

of 3mm (1/8in), then cut three elongated leaves using the scalpel and the template.

12 Thread a 0.5mm (24-gauge) wire up the centre of each leaf, then place on the foam pad and soften the edges with the ball tool. Use the flower veining tool to texture the leaf. Bend the leaf into a natural pose.

13 Wire the leaves to the flower using stem tape. Insert the posy pick into the cake, then insert the flower into this.

Tools & Materials
- Basic flower paste tool kit (see page 14)
- 0.5mm (24-gauge) wire
- Snowdrop petal cutters
- Snowdrop leaf template (see page 138)
- Ball tool
- Floral tape (Nile green)
- Posy pick

Makes three flowers and three leaves
- 42g (1½oz) flower paste
- Yellow pollen powder
- Green paste colour

Inedible flower

If you prefer, the sepal can be made from floral tape in the same shape as the paste sepal.

Tools & Materials
- Basic flower paste tool kit (see page 14)
- Stamens (one per flower)
- 0.5mm (24-gauge) wire
- Floral tape (white)
- Celstick or cocktail stick
- Stephanotis or jasmine or medium star cutter
- Small star cutter
- Ball tool

Makes one flower, one leaf and two buds
- 30g (1oz) flower paste
- Pink dusting powder
- Silver snowflake dusting powder
- Green dusting powder
- Green paste colour

Inedible flower

INTERMEDIATE
37
Stephanotis

Stephanotis floribunda is an evergreen twining vine originally from Madagascar, loved for its intensely fragrant white flowers that are traditionally used in wedding bouquets.

1 Attach a stamen to a 0.5mm (24-gauge) wire using white floral tape.

2 Take a hazelnut-size ball of paste, roll it into a ball and create one of the flowers using the Mexican hat method (see page 24).

3 Roll the flat part of the flower with the Celstick to thin the paste, then thread the cutter over the raised centre and cut out the petals.

4 Hold the flower in your hand and indent the centre with the flower veining tool, then draw the tool up from the centre to part way up each petal, indenting the flower as you go and making the centre larger.

5 Thread the stamen through this centre – but before it goes into the flower, dampen the stamen and pull it into the flower to secure.

6 Leave the flower to dry for 10 minutes, then accentuate the centre and base of the flower with pink dusting powder. Dust with silver snowflake dusting powder.

7 Colour 10g (⅓oz) paste with green paste colour.

Pinch off a pea-size ball, roll out to a thickness of 1–2mm (¹⁄₃₂–¹⁄₁₆in). Cut out a five-pointed star.

8 Place the star on the foam pad and soften the edges with a ball tool, then thread up the back of the stephanotis flower, securing in place with a dot of water.

9 Make the leaf by rolling out more green paste, then cut a rectangle shape with the scalpel and shape one short end to a point. Push a 0.5mm (24-gauge) wire three-quarters of the way down the leaf's length.

10 Place the shape on the foam pad and soften the edges using the ball tool, then score the leaf with the flower veining tool to texture. Bend the leaf into a natural shape. Dust with the green dusting powder to naturalize.

11 Shape the bud by rolling a pea-size pinch of paste to an oval shape, narrower at one end. Take a length of 0.5mm (24-gauge) wire and make a small hook on the end. Insert the wire through the bud, pulling the hook into the paste. Reshape the end, then use the scalpel to score the top with a cross to represent the tightly closed petals.

12 Roll out the remaining white paste into a ribbon shape, approximately 6cm (2½in) long and 13mm (½in) wide. Trim the edges with the scalpel. Indent the edge of the ribbon with the flower veining tool and make a neat row of dots to add interest. Fold the ends of the ribbon to the centre of the ribbon, turn over and pinch the centre. Use the remnants to make another small ribbon to wrap around the centre.

Tools & Materials
- Basic flower paste tool kit (see page 14)
- Rose petal cutters or template (see page 136)
- Cocktail stick
- Ball tool
- Rolled-up kitchen towel

Makes one flower and one leaf
- 30g (1oz) flower paste
- Yellow dusting powder
- Green paste colour

Frangipani
EASY
38

Nothing evokes that tropical feeling quite like the frangipani – their sweet scent and sheer beauty make them universally loved and the blooms look sensational.

1 Roll out three-quarters of the paste to a thickness of 2mm (1/16in).

2 Cut out five petal shapes and place on the foam pad.

3 Use the ball tool to soften the centre of the

petals, but leave the outer edge of the petals thicker.

4 Use the cocktail stick to texture the petals by rolling it backward and forward over the petal.

5 Lay the petals out next to each other, then

moisten the lower edge of each petal with water.

6 Overlap each petal in a fan shape, with the central points of the petals together.

7 Place on the work board and support using a

rolled-up kitchen towel. Leave to firm up.

8 Colour the remaining paste with the green paste colour, cut out the leaf using the petal cutter, then place on the foam pad and soften the edges with the ball tool.

9 Texture the leaf with the flower veining tool, position next to the flower and support with rolled-up kitchen towel until dry.

10 When dry, dust the centre of the flower using yellow dusting powder.

EASY

39 Gerbera

The gerbera comes from the sunflower family, and flowers can be white, yellow, orange, red and pink, so you can experiment with colour schemes. The centre of the flower is sometimes black.

1 Colour 40g (1¼oz) flower paste with the orange paste colour.

2 Roll out the paste to a thickness of 2mm (⅛in) and cut out two of each size of daisy cutter. Work quickly to avoid the paste drying out and cracking.

3 Place the shapes on the foam pad and soften the edges of the petals using the ball tool. Enlarge the centres of the two larger shapes by rolling the ball tool over the centre. Draw the flower veining tool up the centre of each petal to texture.

4 Secure one petal on top of the other using a dot of water. Offset the petals and tweak them using the flower veining tool.

5 Continue building up the flower with two shapes of each size until you have a stack of six shapes.

6 Take a hazelnut-size ball of orange flower paste and flatten to make the flower centre. Prick and pull the paste with the cocktail stick. Dampen lightly with water and dust with the pollen powder.

7 Cut out one of the smallest daisy shapes and prepare as before.

8 Dampen the shape with water then wrap this around the centre that has just been prepared, so the petals curl up the sides.

9 Place this centre on the centre of the prepared stack of daisy shapes, securing with water. Press into the centre and the other petals will curl around it.

10 Dampen the centre of the flower with water and dust with the pollen powder.

11 Colour the remaining paste green for the leaf.

12 Use the leaf cutter to cut out the gerbera leaf Place it on the foam pad, soften the edges with the ball tool, attach to the back of the flower and support until dry.

Tools & Materials

- Basic flower paste tool kit (see page 14)
- Daisy cutters (extra large, large and medium)
- Chrysanthemum leaf cutter
- Ball tool
- Cocktail stick

Makes one flower and one leaf

- 50g (1¾oz) flower paste
- Orange paste colour
- Green paste colour
- Orange pollen powder

The gerbera can
be simplified with
fewer petals to
give pretty, smaller
versions.

Tools & Materials

- Basic flower paste tool kit (see page 14)
- Bone tool
- Cocktail stick
- Stamens
- Floral tape (green)
- 0.5mm (24-gauge) wire
- Circle cutter or holly leaf cutter
- Eight-petal daisy cutters (medium and small)
- Five-petal daisy cutter
- Posy pick

Makes one flower and one leaf
- 30g (1oz) flower paste
- Purple paste colour
- Green paste colour
- Green dusting powder

Inedible flower

ADVANCED

40 Thistle

The emblem of Scotland – this is a simplified way of making a very complex flower.

1 Take a length of 0.5mm (24-gauge) wire and bend over the top.

2 Colour two-thirds of the paste with the purple paste colour. Take a pea-size pinch and shape into a cone. Thread this down the wire, pull the hook into the paste and shape back into a cone. Prick the top of the cone with the cocktail stick to texture.

3 Roll out the purple paste to a thickness of 3mm (⅛in) and cut out a strip 1 x 10cm (½ x 4in). Using the scalpel, cut at right angles along one length of the paste to create a fringe. Cut three-quarters of the way through the width of the paste.

4 Dampen the last quarter of the strip with water, then wrap it around the central cone, working all the way around two to three times to build up the shape of the thistle.

5 Colour the remaining paste with green paste colour. Take a pea-size ball of green paste. Thread it up the wire behind the thistle head.

6 Cut out one five-petal and two eight-petal daisy shapes and place the shapes on the foam pad.

7 Use the bone tool to soften around the daisy petals, drawing the tool up the centre of the petals.

8 Dampen the five-petal shape with water, then thread this up the wire behind the thistle and attach onto the green base, covering the join. Follow this with the two eight-petal daisy shapes, starting with the smaller daisy, making sure that the petal tips are offset.

9 Use the green dusting powder to dust the base of the thistle.

10 Roll out the remaining green paste and cut out the leaf using the holly leaf cutter, or use a circle cutter to cut out small semicircles up and down each side to create a spiky holly-leaf effect. Insert a wire through the leaf's centre.

11 Use the flower veining tool to vein the leaf and bend it into a natural position.

12 Dust the leaf with green dusting powder and attach to the thistle using floral tape. Insert the posy pick into the cake, then insert the flower into this.

Tools & Materials

- Basic flower paste tool kit (see page 14)
- Kusudama cutter (see page 140)
- Ball tool
- Rolled-up kitchen towel
- Cocktail stick

Makes one five-petal flower
- 30g (1oz) flower paste
- Black paste colour (optional)
- Silver snowflake dusting powder (optional)

Origami Kusudama

INTERMEDIATE
41

This design is modelled on the origami kusudama flower made by paper folding.

1 Colour the paste lightly with the black paste colour to give a light gray colour – or leave it white if you prefer.

2 Roll out a hazelnut-size ball of the paste to a thickness of 1mm (1/32in) and cut out one shape with the cutter. Work quickly, as the paste won't fold without cracking when dry.

3 Place the shape on the foam pad and soften the edges using the ball tool.

4 Fold the two triangular wings of the shape towards the centre of the shape. Crease the central point at the base of the shape neatly.

5 Curl the shape into a cone and allow to dry for a few minutes in position.

6 Make either another four petals in the same way for the five-petal flower or another three for the four-petal flower.

7 Join them together at the centre, using water to secure in place. Hold them in your hand and tweak the flower into a suitable position. Use the rolled-up kitchen towel to support if necessary.

8 Once dry, take a pea-size ball of paste, roll It into a ball and flatten with the rolling pin to create a disk.

9 Use the cocktail stick to frill the edge of the disk and attach to the centre of the flower.

10 Take another pea-size ball of paste, flatten it slightly and prick all over the surface with the cocktail stick. Attach to the centre of the flower with water.

11 Dust with silver snowflake dusting powder, if desired.

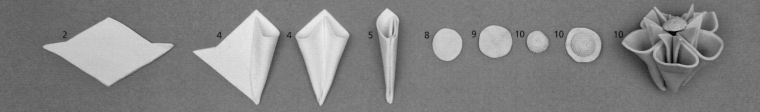

INTERMEDIATE

42 Hibiscus

The hibiscus flower loves warm weather – a perfect flower on the perfect cake for a summer party!

1 Attach a few stamens to the end of a 0.5mm (24-gauge) wire using red floral tape, then work down the wire attaching more stamens, until a length of approximately 1.5cm (⅝in) has been covered.

2 Paint the stamens and the floral tape with red pollen powder and leave to dry.

3 Dampen the end of each stamen with water, then dust over with yellow pollen powder for the pollen effect. Leave to dry for 10 minutes.

4 Colour three-quarters of the flower paste with the pink paste colour and roll out to a thickness of 1mm (¹⁄₃₂in). Cut out five rose-petal shapes and place on the foam pad.

5 Working quickly, soften the edge of the petal with the bone tool, insert one-third of a strand of 0.5mm (24-gauge) wire, frill the edges a little using the bone tool, then texture the petal either with a veiner or by hand using the flower veining tool. Curl the petals on the rolled-up kitchen towel and leave to dry.

6 Dust the centre of the petals with the red dusting powder to create a deep shade of red in the centre of the flower, then blend up the petal. Add in pink dusting powder to further blend the red, finishing with a dusting of silver snowflake dusting powder to give a sparkle.

7 Attach the petals to the central stamen, allowing the stamen to stick out quite prominently, using thin strands of floral tape.

8 Colour the remaining flower paste with green paste colour and roll out to a thickness of 2mm (¹⁄₁₆in). Using the cutter, cut out a heart shape measuring 4 x 2cm (1½ x ¾in). Insert one-third of a length of 0.5mm (24-gauge) wire up the centre of the leaf, stopping three-quarters of the way up.

9 Place the leaf on the foam pad and soften using the ball tool, then score the leaf with the flower veining tool to texture or use the leaf veiner if available. Bend the top over slightly to give a natural appearance.

10 Dust the leaf with the green dusting powder and attach to the stem of the flower with floral tape. Insert the posy pick into the cake, then insert the flowers into this.

Tools & Materials

- Basic flower paste tool kit (see page 14)
- Stamens (10 per flower)
- 0.5mm (24-gauge) wire
- Floral tape (red)
- Rose petal cutter or template (see page 136)
- Bone tool
- Hibiscus veiner (or vein by hand)
- Kitchen towel
- Heart cutter (see page 138)
- General leaf veiner (or vein by hand)
- Posy pick

Makes one flower and three leaves
- 30g (1oz) flower paste
- Red pollen powder
- Yellow pollen powder
- Pink paste colour
- Red dusting powder
- Pink dusting powder
- Silver snowflake dusting powder
- Green paste colour
- Green dusting powder

Inedible flower

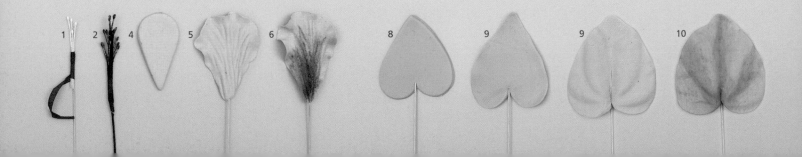

Tools & Materials
- Basic flower paste tool kit (see page 14)
- Blossom cutter (small)
- Ball tool
- 0.5 and 0.3mm (24- and 28-gauge) wire
- Floral tape (Nile green)

Makes 25–30 flowers and three leaves
- 30g (1oz) flower paste
- Green dusting powder

Inedible flower

EASY
43 Lily of the Valley

This is a very delicate-looking flower for spring cakes. It is easy to make using this method and gives a professional finish.

1 Roll out several pea-size balls of flower paste. You need one for each flower and around seven flowers per stem. Attach to 4cm (1½in) of 0.3mm (28-gauge) wire by bending the end over and threading the ball down to the bend. Reshape each ball and let dry for 30 minutes.

2 Repeat the first step but with several bigger balls.

3 Roll out a hazelnut-size ball of the white flower paste to a thickness of 1mm (1/32in). Cut out a blossom for every prepared ball.

4 Place on the foam pad and soften the edges of the blossom with the ball tool. Press the tool into the centre of the blossom and pick up the flower.

5 Dampen the end of the larger balls and press the blossom onto it, indenting the centre of the blossom to give the characteristic lily of the valley appearance, then bend over the head.

6 Wire the flowers and buds together, using thin strands of Nile green floral tape to make the stalks of lily of the valley.

7 Colour 15g (½oz) of flower paste with the green paste colour for the leaves.

8 Roll the paste out to a thickness of 3mm (⅛in) and, using the scalpel, cut out an elliptical shape. Thread a 0.5mm (24-gauge) wire up the centre of the leaf, then place on the foam pad and use the ball tool to soften the edges.

9 Use the flower veining tool to score the leaf to give texture. Bend into a natural position and attach to the flower stems using floral tape. Leave to dry.

10 Dust with green dusting powder to give a natural appearance. Make two more leaves in the same way and attach to the flower stems using floral tape.

Tools & Materials

- Basic flower paste tool kit (see page 14)
- 0.5mm (24-gauge) wire
- Red cotton stamens (four or five per flower)
- Floral tape (green)
- Celstick
- Five-petal daisy cutter (medium)
- Bone tool
- Star cutter
- General leaf cutter or fuchsia leaf template (see page 138)
- General leaf veiner
- Posy pick

Makes five flowers and three leaves
- 30g (1oz) flower paste
- Pink paste colour
- Green paste colour
- Green dusting powder

Inedible flower

Florida Azalea

These flowers are best suited to North and Central Florida gardens and come in a number of varieties. Enjoy making your favourite.

1 Tape four or five stamens onto one-third of a strand of 0.5mm (24-gauge) wire, using floral tape. Allow one of the stamens to protrude further than the others.

2 Colour two-thirds of the flower paste with the pink paste colour.

3 Take a hazelnut-size ball of flower paste, roll and create the flower using the Mexican hat method (see page 24). Roll the flat part of the flower with the Celstick to thin.

Thread the five-petal daisy cutter down over the raised centre and cut out the petals.

4 Hold the flower in your hand and indent the centre with the flower veining tool, then draw the tool up from the centre to part way up each petal, indenting the flower.

5 Turn the flower upside down on the foam pad and draw the ball tool up each petal, curling them back as you work.

6 Thread the prepared stamens through the centre of the flower until the stamens are positioned correctly. Pinch the wire to the base of the flower and smooth until it is flush with the wire to make a neat join.

7 Colour the remaining paste with green paste colour. Roll a hazelnut-size ball and cut out the star shape with the cutter.

8 Soften the star shape on the foam pad with the bone tool, then thread

it up behind the flower, securing it in place with dots of water.

9 Make four flowers in the same way.

10 Roll out the remaining green paste and cut out the leaf shape.

11 Thread a strand of 0.5mm (24-gauge) wire up the centre of the leaf, then use the general leaf veiner to vein the leaf. Curl into a suitable position and leave to dry for one hour.

12 Dust the leaf with the green dusting powder. Make two more leaves.

13 Tape the flowers together in a group, as natural azaleas would be found, adding in the leaves at the back. Use thin strands of floral tape to tape them all together. Insert the posy pick into the cake, then insert the flower into this.

EASY

45 Dogwood

The dogwood is a large, beautiful flower that can be used wired or unwired. It is a simple and elegant flower that looks fabulous on cakes and cupcakes.

1 Roll out a hazelnut-size ball of white paste to a thickness of 3mm (⅛in) and cut out a heart shape using a 3 x 4cm (1¼ x 1½in) cutter.

2 Place on the foam pad. Using the bone tool, soften around the edges of the shape. Work on the top of the petal, broadening the petal and accentuating the indentation of the top.

3 Turn the petal over and soften along the top, curling either side of the indentation back a little.

4 Texture the petal by veining it using the general veiner.

5 Place it back on the foam pad and use the bone tool to frill the edges slightly again. Support on the rolled-up kitchen towel to dry.

6 Make three more petals in the same way.

7 Dust the petal edges lightly with pink dusting powder, then add a slight touch of green in the centre, as shown below. Dust with silver snowflake dusting powder if desired.

8 Construct the petal on the finished cake by applying a dot of white paste in the desired position dampened with water. Then secure the petal points in position.

9 Colour 15g (½oz) of paste with pink paste colour. Then roll 15 small pink balls in different sizes, but not too big.

10 Gently squash them together into a rough cone shape with a flattened top, then secure this in the centre of the petals using water. Dust the flower centre with

pink dusting powder and silver snowflake dust.

11 Colour the remaining white paste with green paste colour. Roll out to a thickness of 1–2mm (¹⁄₃₂–¹⁄₁₆in) and cut out two heart-shaped leaves.

12 Place the leaf on the foam pad, soften with the bone tool, then either use the general leaf veiner or the flower veining tool to vein by hand. Tuck the leaf behind the flower and secure as before.

Tools & Materials

- Basic flower paste tool kit (see page 14)
- Heart cutter or template (see page 138)
- Bone tool
- General veiner (or corn-husk veiner, if available)
- Rolled-up kitchen towel

Makes two flowers
- 30g (1oz) flower paste
- Pink dusting powder
- Silver snowflake dusting powder
- Green dusting powder
- Pink paste colour
- Green paste colour

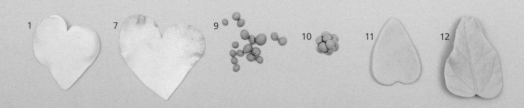

46 Coiled Fantasy Flower

This is a simple coil that can be rolled easily to create beautiful flowers very quickly. You can frill the edge of the paste to create a variation.

1 Colour a pinch of the flower paste with green paste colour and the rest with pink paste colour.

2 Roll out the pink paste to a thickness of 1mm (1/32in), then cut out the coil with the cutter.

3 Start rolling the coil up from the outer end, wrapping it tightly but

being careful not to pinch it together. If you want a frilled flower, use the cocktail stick to soften, thin and frill the edges before coiling up.

4 Coil up the paste until you have reached the size of flower you need and cut off the remaining paste. For a full flower, work right to the end,

then twist the central disk under the whole flower to support the coil.

5 Take a cocktail stick and tweak the petals into a pretty position and leave to dry.

6 Accentuate the petals with a dusting of pink or silver snowflake dusting powder.

7 Using the green paste, shape into little teardrops, seven in total. Flatten them, then use the flower veining tool to texture the centre of the flower.

Tools & Materials
- Basic flower paste tool kit (see page 14)
- Coiled fantasy flower cutter (see page 140)
- Cocktail stick

Makes three large or six small flowers
- 30g (1oz) flower paste
- Green paste colour
- Pink paste colour
- Pink or silver snowflake dusting powder

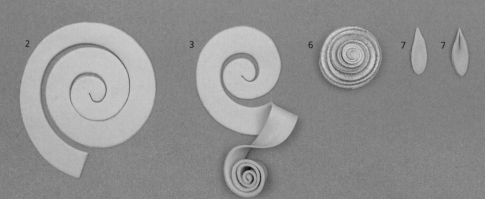

Tools & Materials
- Basic flower paste tool kit (see page 14)
- Blossom and calyx cutters
- Bone tool
- Cocktail stick

Makes three flowers
- 30g (1oz) flower paste
- Yellow paste colour
- Green paste colour
- Silver snowflake dusting powder (optional)

EASY

47 Buttercup

The buttercup is an understated flower, but a group of flower paste versions looks beautiful on a spring-themed cake or cupcake.

1 Colour two-thirds of the flower paste with yellow paste colour.

2 Roll out one third-of the yellow paste to a thickness of 1mm (⅟₃₂in) and cut one flower (you need three, but work one at a time).

3 Place the blossom on the foam pad, soften the edges with the bone tool, then frill slightly.

4 Turn the flower upside down and draw the bone tool lightly up the back of each petal from edge to centre to give a slight curl.

5 Turn the flower back over and indent the centre slightly.

6 Take a small ball of the yellow paste, flatten, then prick with the cocktail stick to texture.

7 Attach the flower centre to the centre of the blossom with water.

8 Colour the remaining paste with the green paste colour. Roll out to a thickness of 1mm (⅟₃₂in) and cut out the calyx.

9 Place this on the foam pad and soften the edges, then attach to the back of the flower, with the points of the calyx between the petals, securing in place with a dot of water.

10 Reroll the green paste and cut out a diamond shape with the scalpel.

11 Cut out the leaf shape by cutting out two triangles from each side, then more smaller triangles of paste at random to give the shredded look.

12 Texture the leaf using the flower veining tool, drawing it down each segment of the leaf.

13 Attach the leaf to the cupcake or cake with a dot of water and place the flower over the top.

14 Dust with silver snowflake dusting powder if desired.

2   3   6   6   8   10    11   12

Tools & Materials

- Basic flower paste tool kit (see page 14)
- Ball tool
- Mini palette knife
- Daisy cutter
- Daisy centre mould
- Rolled-up kitchen towel

Makes one flower
- 34g (1⅛oz) flower paste
- Yellow paste colour
- Silver snowflake dusting powder (optional)

Daisy EASY **48**

A delightful flower with striking colours, the daisy works perfectly adorning a cupcake or as a delicate daisy chain on a larger cake. The fresh colours add a vibrant touch to any summertime celebration cake.

1 Colour 4g (⅛oz) of the flower paste with yellow paste colour and set aside for the daisy centre. Roll out the remaining paste to a thickness of 3mm (⅛in).

2 Cut out a daisy and place it on the foam pad. Soften the paste by lightly pressing it with the ball tool.

3 Press a little more firmly with the ball tool to flatten the shape, broadening the mid-section of each petal. Draw the broad end of the flower veining tool along each petal to curl the edges.

4 Make another daisy shape in the same way.

5 Once you have two completed shapes, glue them together at the centre, offsetting the petals.

6 Roll the yellow flower paste from step 1 into

a ball and push it firmly into the daisy centre mould or sieve (see page 28). Cut off any excess paste using the mini palette knife.

7 Push the paste out of the mould and attach to the centre of the daisy using a dab of water.

8 Leave the finished daisy to dry in the position you want it to hold, supported by a rolled-up kitchen towel.

9 Dust with silver snowflake dusting powder if desired.

Tools & Materials
- Basic flower paste tool kit (see page 14)
- 0.4mm (26-gauge) wire
- Floral stamens (9 per cupcake)
- White floral tape
- Hydrangea flower cutter
- Ball tool
- Posy pick

Makes nine flowers
- 30g (1oz) flower paste
- Blue paste colour
- Green paste colour
- Royal icing
- Dark blue dusting powder

Inedible flower

EASY

49 Hydrangea

Hydrangeas are made up of several small flower heads that work well in flower paste and give a lovely, delicate appearance.

1 Cut a length of 0.4mm (26-gauge) wire into three equal segments and cut a floral stamen in half.

2 Cut a strip of floral tape in half lengthwise to create thin strips of tape. Attach the stamen to the wire using the tape.

3 Colour three-quarters of the paste light blue and the remaining paste green, then roll a tiny ball of light blue flower paste and push the stamen into the ball, securing it with a dot of royal icing.

4 Roll 15g (½oz) light blue flower paste to a thickness of 3mm (⅛in). Cut out a flower shape with the hydrangea cutter. Gently press it out onto the foam pad with a paintbrush.

5 Soften the paste by lightly pressing the ball tool onto the flower. Press more firmly to flatten and thin the shape further. Roll and thin the edges, making the petals larger and thinner.

6 Push the stamen right through the centre of the flower, down to the blue ball, and secure with royal icing. Position the flower and leave to dry for 30 minutes. Make several flowers using this method.

7 Once you have 8 to 10 flower heads, tape them together to form a hydrangea flower. Attach them while some flower heads are still soft to get a more accurate, slightly squashed shape. This gives the hydrangea its compact appearance.

8 Once the flowers have been taped together, add a little dark blue dusting powder in the centre of some of the flower heads or on some of the petals. Insert the posy pick into the cake, then insert the flowers into this.

9 To make the leaves tucked into the display at right, follow the method for Lily of the Valley on page 96.

The leaves can be
attached to the
cupcake with a dot
of royal icing or,
as here, tucked
in between the
suspended cupcakes.

EASY

50 Cherry Blossom

Cherry blossoms flower *en masse*, making the trees look like pink clouds. The cherry flower can be made with a single or double blossom – the double blossoms will create a fuller flower.

1 Tape 8 to 10 stamens to one-third of a strand of 0.5mm (24-gauge) wire, using the green floral tape. Separate the stamens out slightly. These can be white and dusted purple/black, or ready bought in the required colour.

2 Dampen the stamen heads, then dip into the deep red dusting powder to cover the top of the stamen and part of the stamen stem.

3 Roll out a hazelnut-size pinch of white paste to a thickness of 2mm (¹⁄₁₆in), then cut out the blossom shape. Place it on the foam pad and soften the edges with the bone tool. As you soften the petal it will enlarge a

little – run the bone tool around the edge of the petals to frill them.

4 Thread the blossom up behind the prepared stamens, and just before pulling the stamens into the centre of the flower, dampen the centre. Pinch the blossom around the stamens to secure. Hang the stem upside down until dry.

5 Make some flowers with the petals more curled up and others that are more open. If you curl the petal almost together, add the calyx to the back; this will make the bud.

6 Dust pink on the centre of the flower around the base of the stamens.

7 Colour 10g (⅓oz) of paste with green paste colour, take a pea-size ball and create a calyx using the Mexican hat method (see page 24). Use the Celstick to thin the flat part of the calyx further.

8 Thread the calyx cutter down over the raised centre and cut out the calyx.

9 Place on the foam pad and soften slightly.

10 Thread the calyx up behind the flower and secure in place with dots of water.

11 Roll out the remnants of green paste for a leaf, approximately 5 x 2cm (2 x ¾in) and 1mm

(¹⁄₃₂in) thick. Cut out an elliptical shape using the scalpel or leaf template.

12 Place the leaf on the foam pad and soften the edges with the bone tool. Thread one-third of a strand of 0.5mm (24-gauge) wire up the centre of the leaf. Vein the leaf with either the general veiner or by hand using the flower veining tool.

14 Bend into a suitable position to dry.

15 Dust with the green dusting powder to create a realistic-looking leaf.

16 Tape the leaf to the flower stem using floral tape.

The flowers can be
made without calyx
or leaf for a simpler
decoration.

EASY

51 # Clematis

The clematis can be found in many amazing colours, so any variety will blend well when putting together a spray of different flowers to decorate a summer garden cake.

1 Take the cotton thread and wind it loosely around two fingers several times. Take it off your fingers and attach one-third of a strand of wire with a hook on the end around the centre.

2 Bend the threads upward and attach green floral tape over the base of the threads and onto the wire, holding the threads in place. Trim the tops of the threads with scissors.

3 Dust the threads with the yellow dusting powder, then dampen the ends of the threads and dip them into the dusting powder to allow the powder to stick to the threads. Leave to dry.

4 Roll out two-thirds of the flower paste to a thickness of 2mm (1/16in). Cut out five clematis petal shapes and place on the foam pad.

5 Working quickly, soften the edge of the petal with the bone tool, insert one-third of a strand of 0.5mm (24-gauge) wire, frill the edges a little using the bone tool, then texture the petal either with a veiner or by hand using the flower veining tool. Curl the petals as desired and leave to dry.

6 Dust up the centre of the petal with the pink dusting powder to create a deep shade of pink, then blend up the petal, getting fainter as you work up and finishing with a dusting of silver snowflake powder.

7 Attach the petals to the central stamen using thin strands of floral tape.

8 Colour the remaining flower paste with green paste colour and roll out to a thickness of 2mm (1/16in) Cut out the leaf.

Insert one-third of a strand of 0.5mm (24-gauge) wire three-quarters of the way up the centre of the leaf.

9 Place the leaf on the foam pad and soften using the ball tool, then score the leaf with the flower veining tool to texture, or use the veiner. Bend the top over slightly to give a natural look.

10 Dust with the green dusting powder and attach to the flower. Insert the posy pick into the cake, then insert the flower into this.

Tools & Materials

- Basic flower paste tool kit (see page 14)
- White cotton thread on a reel
- Clematis petal and leaf cutter or large lily petal template (see page 136) and leaf template (see page 138)
- Clematis petal veiner (or vein by hand)
- General leaf veiner (or vein by hand)
- Bone tool
- Cocktail stick
- Floral tape (Nile green)
- 0.5mm (24-gauge) wire
- Posy pick

Makes one flower and one leaf
- 30g (1oz) flower paste
- Yellow dusting powder
- Pink dusting powder
- Silver snowflake dusting powder
- Green paste colour
- Green dusting powder

Inedible flower

If making several flowers, make your task easier by leaving out the leaves.

Buttercream Flowers

Coiled Rose EASY 52

Tools & Materials

- Piping bag
- Star piping tube
- Small palette knife

Makes 12 flowers
- Quantity of natural-coloured buttercream (see page 18)
- Red paste colour

A quick and simple way to cover and decorate a cupcake in one go! Use a block-coloured buttercream or try this two-tone effect.

1 In this example the flower is piped onto a sugar paste disk. Prepare the piping bag (see page 20) and insert the star piping tube.

2 Using the palette knife, paint red paste colour thinly down the inside of one side of the bag. Fill the bag with natural-coloured buttercream. This will create the two-tone effect.

3 In one continuous movement, start piping in the centre of the cake or cupcake, then pipe around in a coil shape. Continue until the flower is the desired size.

3

3

3

EASY

53 Rose

A stiffer buttercream gives the frilled edges to the petals, whereas a buttercream that is softer will give a broader petal.

1 In this example the flower is piped onto a sugar paste disk. Colour the buttercream with the red paste colour. Prepare the piping bag (see page 20) and insert the tube.

2 To make a softer buttercream a dash of milk, water or a flavouring, such as orange

juice or vanilla essence, can be added sparingly. If too much liquid is added, thicken the mixture by adding more icing sugar.

3 Pipe a cone in the centre of the cake or cupcake for the centre of the rose.

4 Pipe two semicircular shapes around the cone, angling the tube straight upright.

5 Pipe three semicircular shapes on the next row, angling the top of the tube slightly outward.

6 Pipe five petals on the next row.

7 Continue building up the flower with petals until it is the required size.

Tools & Materials
- Piping bag
- Wilton piping tube no. 104
- Small palette knife

Makes 12 flowers
- Quantity of natural-coloured buttercream (see page 18)
- Red paste colour

3

4

5

6

7

Carnation

A side view of a carnation is a useful flower to add to a repertoire of buttercream flowers for designs on the sides of large cakes.

Tools & Materials
- Piping bags x 2
- Wilton piping tubes no. 104 and no. 3
- Small palette knife

Makes 12 flowers
- Half the quantity of natural-coloured buttercream (see page 18)
- Red paste colour
- Green paste colour

1 Here the flower is piped onto a sugar paste disk. Prepare the piping bag (see page 20) and insert the no. 104 piping tube.

2 Colour a tablespoon of the buttercream with the red paste colour. Using the small palette knife,

smear the red paste down the side of the piping bag, ensuring that the line corresponds with the broad end of the tube. Fill the bag with half of the remaining buttercream.

3 Hold the piping tube with the narrow end

against the cake surface, then pipe in a ruffle effect (a neat zigzag) in an arc shape.

4 Pipe two more rows under the first, overlapping with the previous row and making each row shorter.

5 Prepare the other piping bag and insert the no. 3 tube. Colour the remaining buttercream with the green paste colour and fill the piping bag. Pipe the stalk and a leaf in neat zigzags.

3

4

5

Tools & Materials
- Piping bags x 2
- Wilton piping tubes no. 104 and no. 3
- Small palette knife
- Cocktail stick

Makes 12 flowers
- Half the quantity of natural-coloured buttercream (see page 18)
- Yellow paste colour
- Blue paste colour

Pansy

Choose your favourite colours and pipe a buttercream pansy onto a cupcake for an immediate winner.

1 Here the flower is piped onto a sugar paste disk. Colour half of the buttercream yellow and half blue (or the colours you have chosen). Prepare the piping bag (see page 20), insert the no. 104 tube and fill with yellow buttercream.

2 Pipe two fan shapes close together on the top of the cake or cupcake. Do this by holding the narrow end of the tube on the cake surface and twisting the tube around in an arc, pivoting on the narrow end while squeezing the bag.

3 Repeat this process with two more fan shapes slightly lower and in front of the first two.

4 Prepare the other piping bag, insert the no. 104 tube and fill with blue buttercream.

5 Hold the narrow end of the tube to the base of the yellow buttercream fans, then pipe a fan shape with the blue buttercream. Squeeze the bag firmly to get a good flow of buttercream and a more frilled effect.

6 Finish the flower by using a small amount of yellow buttercream in a bag with the no. 3 tube and piping a circle in the centre of the flower.

7 If necessary, use a cocktail stick to neaten the centre of the flower.

2

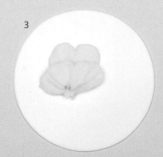

3

5

Tools & Materials
- Piping bags x 3
- Wilton piping tubes
  2 x no. 113 and
  1 x no. 3
- Small palette knife

Makes 12 flowers
- Quantity of natural-coloured buttercream (see page 18)
- Red paste colour
- Green paste colour

Poinsettia

The Christmas poinsettia, a perfect flower to pipe onto a spicy cinnamon cupcake.

1 In this example the flower is piped onto a sugar paste disk. Colour two dessertspoons of buttercream with the red paste colour and two dessertspoons with the green colour.

2 Prepare two piping bags (see page 20) and insert the no. 113 tubes.

3 Fill one piping bag with the red buttercream and the other piping bag with the green buttercream.

4 Start piping the red bracts on the outside edge of the flower in a circular shape.

5 On the first row, pipe a few green leaves intermingled with the red bracts. The bracts are formed by holding the bag at a 45-degree angle to the cake or cupcake surface, with the flat of the tube resting on the cake surface. Start squeezing the piping bag while drawing the tube up and away from the cake

or cupcake. Stop squeezing and pull the bag away to create the bract or leaf.

6 Continue all the way around the flower, creating a circle of bracts, then start a row on the inside of the first, continuing until the whole flower is filled with bracts.

7 Prepare the third piping bag, insert the no. 3 tube and fill with the remaining green buttercream.

8 Pipe dots in the centre of the flower.

4

7

8

ADVANCED

57 # Chrysanthemum

This flower is well worth the effort in trying to master the technique. Once mastered, it is effective for lots of flowers with tiny clusters of petals.

1 In this example the flower is piped onto a sugar paste disk. Colour the buttercream with the purple paste colour.

2 Prepare the piping bag (see page 20) and insert the piping tube.

3 Fill the piping bag with the purple buttercream.

4 Pipe the outside edge of the flower on the cake's surface, in a circular shape made up of short petals.

5 The petals are formed by holding the bag at a 45-degree angle to the cake or cupcake surface, with the centre of the horseshoe-shaped tube resting on the surface. Start squeezing the piping bag while drawing the tube up and away from the cake or cupcake. Stop squeezing and pull the bag away to create the petal.

6 Continue all the way around the flower, creating a circle of petals, then start a row on the inside of the first, continuing and building up the petals to create the flower.

7 If you make a mistake or are not happy with the effect, simply scrape the buttercream off the cake with a palette knife and start again!

4

6

6

Tools & Materials

- Piping bags x 2
- Wilton piping tubes no. 104 and no. 3
- Small palette knife

Makes 12 flowers
- Half the quantity of natural-coloured buttercream (see page 18)
- Yellow paste colour

Daisy

An easy flower for a beginner to pipe, good as a single flower on a cake or as several flowers piped together.

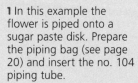

1 In this example the flower is piped onto a sugar paste disk. Prepare the piping bag (see page 20) and insert the no. 104 piping tube.

2 Fill the piping bag with three-quarters of the natural buttercream.

3 Pipe the first petal by placing the narrow end of the piping tube on the cupcake or cake surface. Squeeze the bag while drawing the large end of the tube up and down in an 'n' shape. This will create the petal. Make the shape very narrow to emulate the shape of a daisy petal.

4 Repeat this process seven more times to create an eight-petal flower, making sure that the centre of each petal is at the same point.

5 Colour the remaining buttercream with the yellow paste colour. Prepare the other piping bag, insert the no. 3 tube and add the yellow buttercream. Pipe a small coil first, then pipe dots on top of the coil for the flower centre.

Tools & Materials

- Piping bags x 2
- Wilton piping tubes no. 104 and no. 3
- Small palette knife
- Cocktail stick

Makes 12 flowers
- Quantity of natural-coloured buttercream (see page 18)
- Yellow paste colour

INTERMEDIATE

59

Daffodil

Spring is here when daffodils appear – freshly baked cupcakes with a daffodil head on each, so inspiring!

1 In this example the flower is piped onto a sugar paste disk. Colour the buttercream with the yellow paste colour.

2 Prepare the piping bag (see page 20), insert the no. 104 tube and fill with three-quarters of the yellow buttercream.

3 Pipe the first petal by placing the narrow end of the tube on the cake surface. Squeeze the bag while drawing the large end up and down in an 'n' shape. This will create the petal shape. Make the shape quite narrow.

4 Repeat this process four more times to create a five-petal flower, making sure that the centre of each petal is at the same point.

5 Prepare the other bag, insert the no. 3 tube and fill with the remaining yellow buttercream.

6 Pipe a small ring around the centre of the petals. Continue piping over the same ring several times to build up for the trumpet of the flower.

7 Take the cocktail stick and lightly pull out the final ring just piped to give a frilled edge.

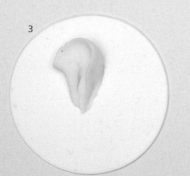
3

4

6

7

Tools & Materials

- Piping bags x 2
- Wilton piping tube no. 3
- Small palette knife

Makes 12 flowers
- Half the quantity of natural-coloured buttercream (see page 18)
- Pale green paste colour
- Purple paste colour

Bluebell

A delicate nodding flower that would look perfect on the side of a cake with other bluebells in a row.

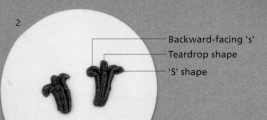

2

Backward-facing 's'
Teardrop shape
'S' shape

1 Colour half of the buttercream pale green and half purple.

2 Prepare the piping bag (see page 20), insert the no. 3 tube and fill with the purple buttercream. The flower is made up of three piped petals. Pipe the first petal in an elongated 's' shape. Pipe the middle petal by piping a thick teardrop. Finish the flower by piping the third petal as a backward 's', so that it mirrors the first petal.

3 Pipe through the centre of the two shapes, giving depth to the centre of the flower.

4 Prepare the other piping bag, insert the no. 3 piping tube and fill with the green buttercream. Pipe the sepal on the flower, then the stalk and, finally, a leaf.

4

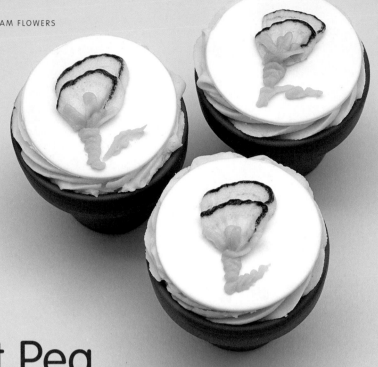

Tools & Materials
- Piping bags x 2
- Wilton piping tubes no. 104 and no. 3
- Small palette knife

Makes 12 flowers
- Quantity of natural-coloured buttercream (see page 18)
- Purple paste colour
- Green paste colour

INTERMEDIATE

61 Sweet Pea

String groups of sweet peas together on the side of a cake for a quick but effective decoration.

1 Here the flower is piped onto a sugar paste disk. Prepare the piping bag (see page 20) and insert the no. 104 piping tube.

2 Using the palette knife, smear a small amount of the purple paste colour down the side of the piping bag, ensuring that the line corresponds with the broad end of the piping tube.

3 Fill the piping bag with three-quarters of the natural buttercream.

4 Hold the piping tube with the narrow end against the cake surface, squeeze the bag and draw the tube around in a semicircle – this will create a fan shape with a dark purple edge.

5 Repeat the previous step to overlay a second petal; however, move the tube down 6mm by (¼in) to allow the petal to be piped slightly lower than the first.

6 Colour the remaining buttercream with green paste colour. Prepare the other piping bag, insert the no. 3 tube and add the green buttercream.

7 Pipe the sepal and stalk, with a little leaf to finish.

4

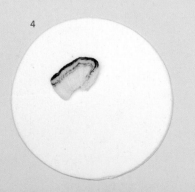

5

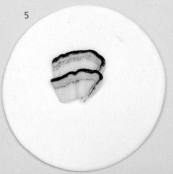

7

Tools & Materials

- Piping bags x 2
- Wilton piping tubes no. 104 and no. 3
- Small palette knife

Makes 36 flowers
- Quantity of natural-coloured buttercream (see page 18)
- Pink paste colour
- Yellow paste colour

Apple Blossom INTERMEDIATE 62

Put clusters of three apple blossoms on each cupcake, overlapping their petals.

1 Here the flower is piped onto a sugar paste disk. Prepare the piping bag (see page 20) and insert the no. 104 tube.

2 Using the small palette knife, smear a small amount of the pink paste colour down the side of the piping bag, ensuring that the line corresponds with the broad end of the piping tube.

3 Fill the piping bag with all but two dessertspoons of natural buttercream.

4 Pipe the first petal by placing the narrow end of the piping tube on the cake surface. Squeeze the bag while drawing the large end of the tube up and down in an 'n' shape. This will create the petal.

5 Repeat this process four times to create a five-petal flower, making sure that the centre of each petal is at the same point.

6 Colour the remaining buttercream with the yellow paste colour. Prepare the other piping bag, insert the no. 3 tube and add the yellow buttercream. Pipe dots in the centre of the flower.

Tools & Materials

- Piping bags x 2
- Wilton piping tubes no. 104 and no. 3
- Cocktail stick
- Small palette knife

Makes 12 flowers
- Quantity of natural-coloured buttercream (see page 18)
- Red paste colour
- Black paste colour
- Black nonpareils (optional)

EASY

63 Poppy

A striking red flower with black nonpareils sprinkled in the centre to form the whorl of stamens.

1 In this example the flower is piped onto a sugar paste disk. Colour all but three tablespoons of buttercream red.

2 Prepare the piping bag (see page 20), insert the no. 104 tube and fill the piping bag with the red buttercream.

3 Pipe the first petal by placing the narrow end of the piping tube on the cake surface. Squeeze the bag while drawing the large end up and down in an 'n' shape. This will create the petal shape.

4 Repeat this process four more times to create a five-petal flower, making sure that the centre of each petal is at the same point.

5 Colour the remaining buttercream with the black paste colour. Prepare the other piping bag, insert the no. 3 tube and add the black buttercream. Fill in the centre of the poppy by piping black dots, and if desired, sprinkle with black nonpareils.

Tools & Materials

- Piping bags x 2
- Wilton piping tubes no. 81 and no. 3
- Small palette knife

Makes 12 flowers
- Quantity of natural-coloured buttercream (see page 18)
- Brown paste colour
- Yellow paste colour

Sunflower

ADVANCED

To recreate the sunflower requires some skills with a piping bag, but this technique is one that's worth mastering.

1 In this example the flower is piped onto a sugar paste disk. Colour three tablespoons of the buttercream brown and the rest yellow.

2 Prepare the piping bag (see page 20), insert the no. 81 tube and fill the piping bag with yellow buttercream.

3 Start piping the outside edge of the flower on the top of the cake or cupcake, in a circular shape made up of short petals.

4 The petals are formed by holding the bag at a 45-degree angle to the cake or cupcake surface, with the centre of the horseshoe-shaped tube resting on the surface. Start squeezing the piping bag while drawing the tube up and away from the cake or cupcake. Stop squeezing and pull the bag away to create the petal.

5 Continue all the way around the flower, creating a circle of petals,

then start a row on the inside of the first, continuing for three or four rows.

6 Prepare the other piping bag, insert the no. 3 tube and add the brown buttercream. Pipe thick dots all over the centre of the flower.

3

6

Tools & Materials
• Piping bags x 2
• Wilton piping tube no. 3
• Small palette knife

Makes 12 flowers
• Half the quantity of natural-coloured buttercream (see page 18)
• Green paste colour
• Purple paste colour

EASY

65 Lavender

Purple paste colour perfectly captures the lovely shade of lavender.

1 Here the flower is piped onto a sugar paste disk. Colour all but three dessertspoons of buttercream with the green paste colour.

2 Prepare the piping bag (see page 20), insert the no. 3 tube and fill the piping bag with green buttercream.

3 Pipe long, sweeping green lines on the top of the cupcake or cake. This flower requires a smooth, flat surface.

4 Pipe little green teardrop shapes up the stalk for the random leaves on the lavender stalk.

5 Colour the remaining buttercream with the purple paste colour. Prepare the other piping bag, insert the no. 3 tube and add the purple buttercream.

6 Pipe little purple teardrops randomly up the stalks for the lavender flowers.

3

4

6

Tools & Materials

- Piping bags x 2
- Wilton piping tubes no. 104 and no. 3
- Small palette knife

Makes 12 flowers
- Half the quantity of natural-coloured buttercream (see page 18)
- Green paste colour
- Yellow paste colour

Zinnia ADVANCED **66**

Zinnias comes in so many colours – try making several different shades for a truly colourful cupcake display.

1 In this example the flower is piped onto a sugar paste disk. Colour all but two dessertspoons of the buttercream with the green paste colour.

2 Prepare the piping bag (see page 20), insert the no. 104 tube and fill the piping bag with green buttercream.

3 Pipe the first petal by placing the narrow end of the piping tube on the cake surface. Squeeze the bag while drawing the large end up and down in an 'n' shape. This will create the petal shape.

4 Repeat this process nine times to create a 10-petal flower, making sure that the centre of each petal is at the same point.

5 Pipe the next row right on top of the first from the centre, making the petals shorter.

6 Create a third row on top of the others, making it shorter still, so that the three layers are clear.

7 Colour the remaining buttercream with the yellow paste colour. Prepare the other piping bag, insert the no. 3 tube and add the yellow buttercream. Pipe dots in the centre of the flower.

Royal Icing Flowers

Orchid ADVANCED **67**

As well as piping these flowers directly onto the cake, pipe them onto squares of greaseproof paper. The flowers will then dry and can be applied to any part of the cake by securing with a dot of royal icing.

1 Colour the royal icing with the pink paste colour.

2 Prepare the piping bag and insert the no. 104 tube.

3 Using the small palette knife, fill the piping bag with pink royal icing.

4 Pipe the first petal by placing the narrow end of the piping tube on the cake surface. Squeeze the bag while drawing the broad end up and round in a fan shape.

5 Repeat this process twice more in a triangle shape to create a three-petal shape, making sure that the centre of each petal is at the same point.

6 Hold the shape with a petal pointing away from you; the next two petals are going to be piped in between this petal, as shown below.

7 Turn the flower upside down and pipe a fan shape at the base, but make this much fuller. Leave to dry for 24 hours.

8 Use the paintbrush to paint the centre of the orchid with pink paste colour to accentuate the centre of the petals.

4   5   6   7

INTERMEDIATE

68 Wild Rose

The wild rose can be piped in an array of colours. Try piping it in white and dusting the edges in pink to give a delicate appearance.

1 Colour the royal icing with the yellow paste colour. Prepare the piping bag and insert the no. 103 tube.

2 Using the small palette knife, fill the piping bag with all but two dessertspoons of the yellow royal icing.

3 Place the tube with the broad end on the piping surface and pipe an 'n' shape, while moving the narrow end a little to create the petal.

4 Pipe four more petals to create the flower.

5 Darken the colour of the remaining royal icing by adding more paste colour. Fill a piping bag, snip the tip off the bag and pipe dots in the flower centre.

Tools & Materials

- Piping bags x 2
- Wilton piping tube no. 103
- Small palette knife

Makes 40 flowers
- One-quarter quantity of royal icing (see page 19)
- Yellow paste colour

3

4

4

4

5

5

Tools & Materials

- Piping bag
- Wilton piping tube no. 3
- Rolling pin
- Rose petal cutter
- Small palette knife
- Paintbrush

Makes 12 flowers
- 30g (1oz) flower paste
- Peach paste colour
- One-quarter quantity of royal icing (see page 19)
- Alcohol (vodka)
- Silver snowflake dusting powder

Fantasy Daisy

This is a good flower to start with because the pieces are dried flat and then constructed into the flower.

1 Colour the flower paste with peach paste colour. Roll out the paste to a thickness of 1mm (1/32in) Use the rose petal cutter to cut out seven petals for the flower and dry them flat.

2 Colour all the royal icing with peach paste colour.

Prepare the piping bag and insert the no. 3 tube. Using the small palette knife, fill the bag with royal icing. Pipe a line of royal icing around the curved edge of the petal.

3 Take a damp paintbrush (dampen with water but dry a little first – it must

not be dripping) and, before the royal icing sets, draw the brush through the soft royal icing.

4 Pipe a second line of royal icing a little below the first, repeating the brushing with the damp paintbrush. You can do this two or three times on

each petal, depending on the effect you want to create. Leave to dry.

5 Mix a paste using the alcohol and silver snowflake dust. Use the paste to paint the white flecks onto the petals.

6 Pipe a large dot of royal icing where you want the centre of the flower to be. Attach the petals in a fan shape, securing in place with royal icing on the back as you work. Pipe a centre to the flower. Dust with silver snowflake dusting powder if you wish.

1

2

3

5

70 Ox-eye Daisy

A just-picked white daisy with a bright yellow centre. Pipe the flower directly into position. If you make a mistake, simply scrape the icing off with a palette knife and start again!

1 Prepare the piping bag and insert the no. 127 tube.

2 Using the small palette knife, fill the piping bag with white royal icing. Reserve a small amount for the flower centres.

3 Pipe the first petal by placing the broad end of the piping tube on the cake surface. Squeeze the bag while drawing the narrow end up and round in an 'n' shape.

4 Continue working around the flower, one petal at a time, until the whole circle of petals is complete – 10 in total.

5 Colour the remaining royal icing with the yellow paste colour. Fill a piping bag with yellow royal icing, snip the tip off the piping bag and pipe the dots in the centre of the flower.

Tools & Materials

- Piping bags x 2
- Wilton piping tube no. 127
- Small palette knife

Makes 50 flowers
- One-quarter quantity of royal icing (see page 19)
- Yellow paste colour

3   4   4   4   5

Cactus Blossom

Set the cactus blossom against a pastel-coloured sugar paste background to make its subtle charms stand out.

Tools & Materials

- Piping bags x 2
- Wilton piping tube no. 69
- Small palette knife

Makes 30 flowers
- One-quarter quantity of royal icing (see page 19)

1 Prepare the piping bag and insert the no. 69 tube. Using the small palette knife, fill the bag with white royal icing. Reserve a small amount for the flower centre.

2 Place the tube on the piping surface and squeeze the bag, at the same time lifting the tube up and out. Stop squeezing and pull the tube away, leaving a petal shape.

3 Continue in the same way, creating a ring of petals.

4 Work another two rows inside the first.

5 Finish the blossom off by filling a bag with the remaining white royal icing, snip the tip off the bag and pipe dots into the centre of the flower.

Tools & Materials

- Piping bags x 2
- Wilton piping tube no. 103
- Small palette knife

Makes 50 flowers
- One-quarter quantity of royal icing (see page 19)
- Blue paste colour
- Green paste colour

EASY

72 Flax

An unusual flower to include in a book on sugar flowers, but there are so few blue subjects that this one had to be featured. It's pretty and easy to make.

1 Colour all but two tablespoons of the royal icing with the blue paste colour. Prepare the piping bag and insert the no. 103 tube.

2 Using the small palette knife, fill the piping bag with blue royal icing.

3 Pipe the first petal by placing the broad end of the piping tube on the cake surface. Hold the tube quite upright. Squeeze the bag while drawing the narrow end up and round in an 'n' shape.

4 Continue working around the flower, one petal at a time, until the whole circle of petals is complete – five in total.

5 Colour the remaining royal icing with the green paste colour. Fill a piping bag with green royal icing, snip the tip off the piping bag and pipe the dots in the centre of the flower.

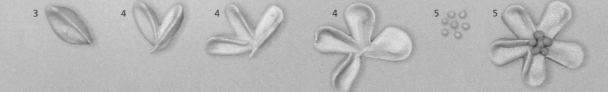

Tools & Materials

- Piping bags x 2
- Wilton piping tube no. 103
- Small palette knife

Makes 50 flowers
- One-quarter quantity of royal icing (see page 19)
- Pink paste colour
- Yellow paste colour
- Silver snowflake dusting powder

Alpine Blossom

INTERMEDIATE

73

A crisp, fresh blossom to pipe that requires a little more skill, as the petals overlay each other – but it is definitely worth the effort.

1 Prepare the piping bag and insert the no. 103 tube.

2 Using the small palette knife, smear a small amount of the pink paste colour down the side of the piping bag, ensuring that the line corresponds with the narrow end of the piping tube.

3 Fill the piping bag with white royal icing. Reserve two tablespoons for the flower centres.

4 Pipe the first petal by placing the broad end of the piping tube on the cake surface. Squeeze the bag while drawing the narrow end up and round in a fan shape.

5 Repeat this process four times to create a five-petal flower, making sure that the centre of each petal is at the same point.

6 Colour the remaining royal icing with the yellow paste colour. Fill a piping bag with yellow royal icing, snip the tip off the piping bag and pipe the dots in the centre of the flower.

7 When the flower is dry, dust with silver snowflake dusting powder.

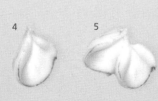

4   5   6   6   6

EASY
74 Trillium

A pretty frilled flower, and the frilled effect is easy to create!

1 Prepare the piping bag and insert the no. 104 tube.

2 Using the small palette knife, fill the piping bag with white royal icing. Reserve a small amount for the flower centres.

3 Place the tube with the narrow end on the piping surface and pipe a fan shape, undulating the bag at the same time to get a rippled effect.

4 Pipe two more petals to create a three-petal flower.

5 Colour the remaining royal icing with the yellow paste. Fill a piping bag with yellow royal icing, snip the tip off the piping bag and pipe three large dots in the centre of the flower.

Tools & Materials

- Piping bags x 3
- Wilton piping tube no. 104
- Small palette knife

Makes 45 flowers
- One-quarter quantity of royal icing (see page 19)
- Purple paste colour
- Yellow paste colour
- Orange paste colour

Viola INTERMEDIATE 75

If you're not sure of your piping skills, pipe this flower onto a small square of greaseproof paper and leave to dry. The purple icing will stain whatever it touches and can't be removed.

1 Colour half the royal icing with the purple paste colour. Prepare the piping bag and insert the no. 104 tube. Using the small palette knife, fill the piping bag with purple royal icing.

2 Place the tube with the broad end on the piping surface and pipe an 'n' shape while moving the narrow end slightly to create the petal. Repeat.

3 Wash the tube. Colour the other half of the royal icing with the yellow paste colour, reserving a small amount for the flower centres. Prepare a new bag, insert the tube and fill with yellow royal icing.

4 Pipe two petals either side of the purple petals, using the same technique.

5 Pipe the base petal by placing the narrow end of the piping tube at the centre of the flower and squeezing the piping bag while moving the narrow end in an 'n' shape, moving the piping bag up and down to get a frilled effect.

6 Colour the remaining royal icing with the orange paste colour. Fill a piping bag with orange royal icing, snip the tip off the piping bag and pipe a dot in the flower centre.

2   2   4   4   6

Templates

If you don't have the specific cutters required, use these templates to create several of the flowers and leaves in the book. Trace the flowers onto card or plastic (for example, ice-cream or margarine containers) and cut the shape out with scissors.

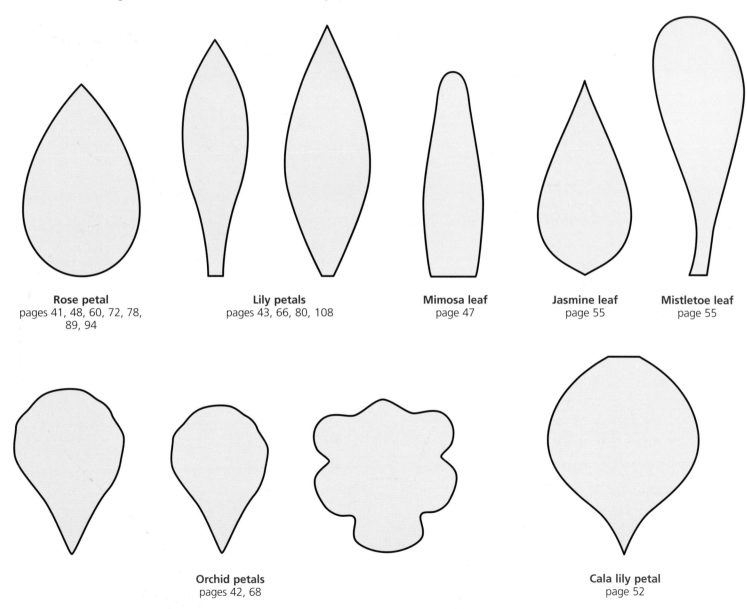

Rose petal
pages 41, 48, 60, 72, 78,
89, 94

Lily petals
pages 43, 66, 80, 108

Mimosa leaf
page 47

Jasmine leaf
page 55

Mistletoe leaf
page 55

Orchid petals
pages 42, 68

Cala lily petal
page 52

Peony petal
page 44

Anemone petal
pages 54, 75

Bindweed petal
page 58

Ivy leaf
page 62

Anthurium petal
page 53

Dogwood leaf
page 98

Dogwood petal
page 98

Bramble leaf
pages 72, 78, 82

Fuchsia leaf
pages 82, 97

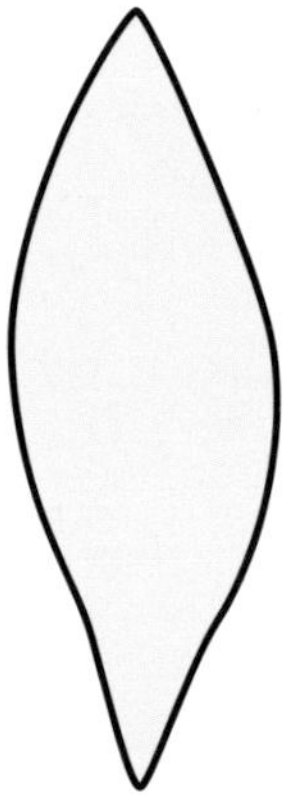

Cherry blossom leaf
page 106

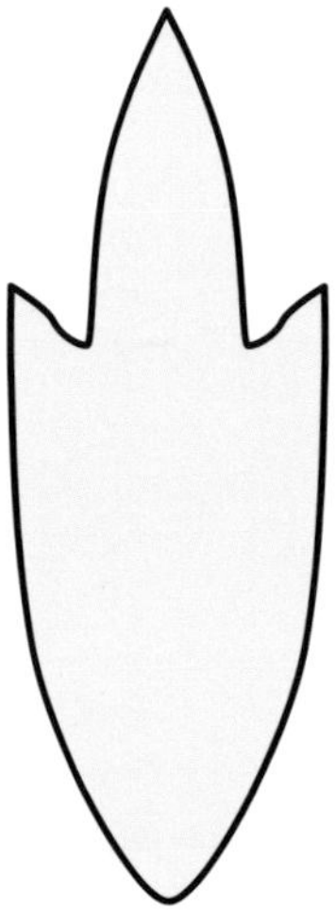

Clematis
page 108

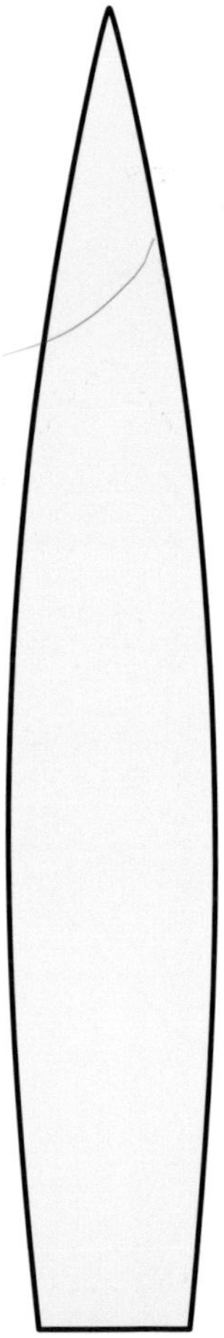

Snowdrop leaf
page 86

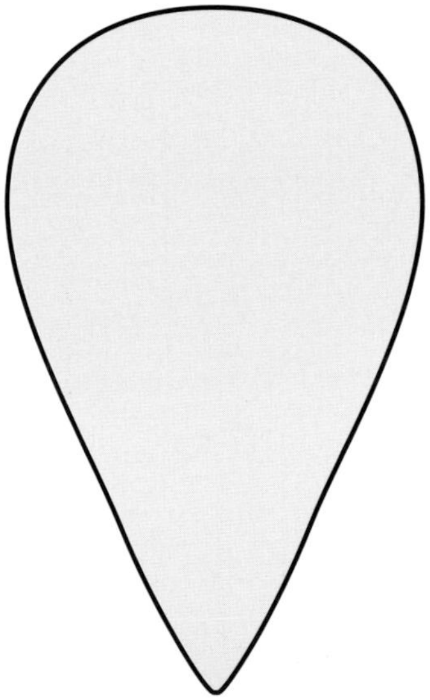

Hibiscus petal
page 94

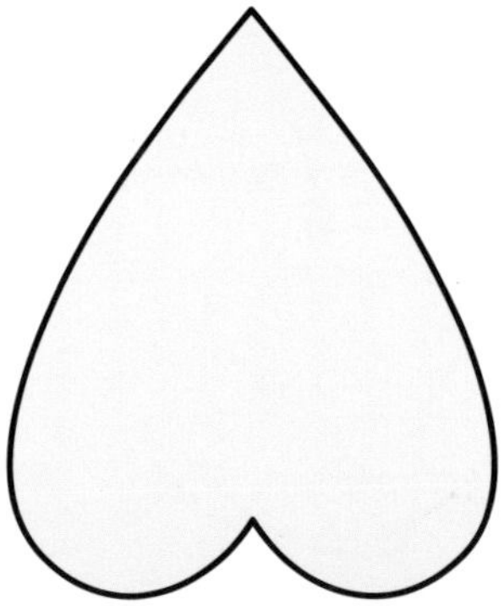

Hibiscus leaf
page 94

Azalea leaf
page 97

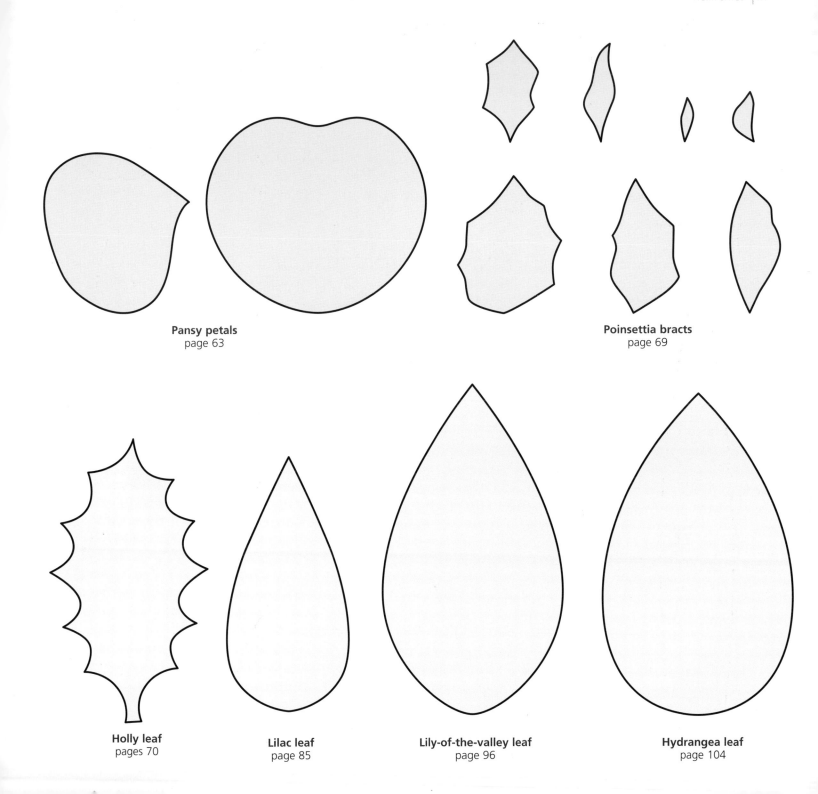

Pansy petals
page 63

Poinsettia bracts
page 69

Holly leaf
pages 70

Lilac leaf
page 85

Lily-of-the-valley leaf
page 96

Hydrangea leaf
page 104

Resources

Squires Kitchen
www.squires-shop.com
International postage available
T: +44 (0)1252 260 260
e: customer@squires-shop.com

Flower paste, royal icing powder, marzipan, modelling chocolate, dusting powders and paste, liquid and gel food colours.

Too Nice To Slice
www.toonicetoslice.co.uk
International postage available
T: +44 (0)7880 701732
e: toonicetoslicebyhelenpenman@gmail.com

Helen Penman cutters (including the kusudama and coil flower cutters), cupcake wrappers and more available in the Online Store.

Kit Box
www.kitbox.co.uk
T: +44 (0)1275 879 030
e: support@kitbox.info

Metal cutters, ribbon cutters and general cake-decorating supplies.

CelCakes & CelCrafts
www.celcrafts.com
T: +44 (0)1759 371447
e: sales@celcrafts.com

Cake-decorating tools.

Hawthorne Hill
www.hawthornehill.co.uk
T: +44 (0)7905 811505
e: Via contact form on website.

Orchid and other flower cutters, moulds and tools.

Fancy Flours
www.fancyflours.com
T: +1 (406) 587 0118
e: info@fancyflours.com

General baking supplies.

Wilton
www.wilton.com
T: +1 888 373 4588
e: Via contact form on website.

Cake-decorating tools, cutters, piping tubes and piping bags.

Index

Acknowledgements

All step-by-step and other images are the copyright of Quarto Publishing plc. While every effort has been made to credit contributors, Quarto would like to apologize should there have been any omissions or errors – and would be pleased to make the appropriate correction for future editions of the book.

Author's acknowledgements

I have been very fortunate that Squires Kitchen in Farnham, Surrey, have liked my cake designs over the years and featured them in their magazines, written two books with me, and they also supplied the pastes for the flowers in this book. I am very grateful to Beverley and Jenny at Squires for their support. I have also been so blessed to have such an amazing publishing team at Quarto – Kate, Ruth and Emma – without whom this book wouldn't be!